T0007204

Leave No One Behind

*Daily Meditations for Military Service Members
and Veterans in Recovery*

Hazelden
Publishing

Hazelden Publishing
Center City, Minnesota 55012
hazelden.org/bookstore

978-1-61649-918-1

Library of Congress Cataloging-in-Publication Data

Names: Hazelden Publishing.
Title: Leave no one behind : daily meditations for military service members and
    veterans in recovery.
Description: Center City, Minnesota : Hazelden Publishing, 2022. | Includes
    index. | Summary: "A daily meditation book for service members who are in
    recovery, with each meditation written by a service member or veteran in
    recovery"— Provided by publisher.
Identifiers: LCCN 2022002888 (print) | LCCN 2022002889 (ebook) |
    ISBN 9781616499181 (paperback) | ISBN 9781616499198 (epub)
Subjects: LCSH: Recovering addicts—Meditations. | Recovering alcoholics—
    Meditations. | Soldiers—Meditations. | Veterans—Meditations. | Affirmations. |
    Devotional calendars.
Classification: LCC BL625.9.R43 L43 2022 (print) | LCC BL625.9.R43 (ebook) |
    DDC 204/.42—dc23/eng20220318
LC record available at https://lccn.loc.gov/2022002888
LC ebook record available at https://lccn.loc.gov/2022002889

This publication is not intended as a substitute for the advice of health care
professionals.

Hazelden Publishing offers a variety of information on addiction and related areas.
Our publications do not necessarily represent Hazelden Betty Ford Foundation's
programs, nor do they officially speak for any Twelve Step organization.

Alcoholics Anonymous, AA, and the Big Book are registered trademarks of
Alcoholics Anonymous World Services, Inc.

COVER DESIGN: TERRI KINNE
TYPESETTING: PERCOLATOR GRAPHIC DESIGN
DEVELOPMENTAL EDITORS: ANDREA LIEN,
KAI BENSON, AND MARC OLSON
EDITORIAL PROJECT MANAGER: BETTY CHRISTIANSEN

Acknowledgments

Brian and Marlene Dooner

Dooner Social Ventures

Tim Joyce and Corlan Strategies

Kate Sperber

Kim Tapia, Polanko Group

Dijonna Wagner

Capt. Jeff Horwitz, JAGC, USN (Ret.), Chief Operating Officer, SAFE Project

Col. Scott Jensen, USMC (Ret.), President and Owner, Alpine Global Solutions

Hazelden Betty Ford Foundation Strategic Innovation Fund

Alta DeRoo, MD, Chief Medical Officer, Hazelden Betty Ford Foundation

Quyen Ngo, PhD, LP, Executive Director of the Butler Center for Research, Hazelden Betty Ford Foundation

Jacqueline Braughton, PhD, LAMFT, Research Scientist, Hazelden Betty Ford Foundation

Jeremiah Gardner, Director of Communications and Public Affairs, Hazelden Betty Ford Foundation

Thank you to all the contributors, facilitators, writers, designers, promoters, and editors who worked so hard to make this book.

Introduction

Meditation books have helped millions of people as they've made their way through recovery from substance use disorders and addiction. Ever since our first one, *Twenty-Four Hours a Day*, was published in 1954, Hazelden Publishing has created almost fifty of these books of daily inspiration. Some are for people who are in recovery from alcohol use; some are for people with other drug addictions. Over the years, we've published books tailored to a number of different demographic groups, but until now, we hadn't created one for people who have served in the military. We knew it was time to create a meditation book specifically for service members and veterans in recovery. And we knew that you should be the ones to write it.

We sent out the call for help and were in awe of the people who answered it. Some wrote their own meditations, and some told us their stories out loud so we could write their experiences to share with you here. We have included veterans and service members of different ages and from different eras of the military. There are men and women of various backgrounds, cultures, branches, ranks, and positions. These people have had experiences with both alcohol and drugs as well as many successes among their attempts at recovery—all of which help us relate to their journeys. Some of them share their histories of pain and trauma—physical, emotional, sexual— before, during, and after their time in the military. We do not shy away from any of these stories, because they are more common than many of us realize. If even one of the 366 meditations in this book finds someone who needs to read it, we have succeeded.

When we first started asking veterans to help us write this book, they expressed some very valid skepticism that the stories and meditations might be filtered to make them more digestible by civilians—that the stories of what people went through when they served could be too graphic. This makes a lot of sense. Multiple contributors have mentioned that their time in the military is not something that people who haven't experienced it can understand.

So we were careful to make sure people knew that they could share their stories as honestly as if they were in a meeting with their fellow veterans, the insiders. There would be no judgment from us. This book doesn't need to help anyone but the people who have been there—or still are. This is your book. And just as important as what's written are the messages are that aren't spelled out in words. As graphic as these written accounts may be, for the people who've lived these stories, what's left unsaid is just as impactful. If you've lived some of the same experiences as the contributors in this book, you can read between the lines. That's what happens when you tell your stories to people who are like you. You get it. You already know the context and all of the shared language. You can picture what's been written. It is powerful, it is real, and it is validating.

This is not just a book that will help people; it is a piece of history. Its existence is a testament to how we need to be there for the people who have served our country—

and the citizens of the world—because of the unique conditions you have faced . . . and continue to face.

There are different ways to read this book. You can read one meditation a day as a check-in and daily inspiration or read them all at once if you need a rapid infusion of insight from people who served with you and are recovering with you. We followed the fellowship tradition of using first names with last initials so you can see who contributed each of the meditations as well as their branch and years in the service. You'll find all sorts of themes throughout the meditations, including how to manage your memories, how to relate to your families, how to fight stigma, and how to suit up and show up for yourselves. On a broader level, you'll also learn more about how to figure out that you need help, how to ask for it, and how you can help others.

As Kenneth B. says in his August 18 meditation "We Are Not Alone," "One of the biggest things in the military is that there's not one mission that gets done by itself. It's a team effort. You win together, and you lose together. Same for recovery."

We want to extend heartfelt gratitude to all of the service members and veterans who made this mission and book possible.

Thank you,
The editors

Foreword

One thing we know for sure about addiction is that it does not discriminate. Every human being carries some risk for developing a substance use disorder. No amount of career or financial success insulates us. No fine-tuned moral compass. And no military rank, either. In fact, high-stress jobs can be a risk factor.

As a Naval Flight Officer who led major combat and humanitarian missions around the globe and an obstetrician-gynecologist who helped bring thousands of babies into the world, I grew accustomed to extraordinary, pressure-filled situations. But that didn't prevent me from developing a substance use disorder, just like so many millions of others do every year. Today, I am grateful because it was my substance use disorder that led me to recovery and to a renewed spirit of service, love, and connection that, to this day, aligns closely with the esprit de corps I so cherished in the military.

When Hazelden Publishing invited me to write the foreword for *Leave No One Behind,* I was both elated and humbled. Not only was it a chance to share my story of hope and healing but also a unique opportunity to connect again with my brothers, sisters, shipmates, and battle buddies.

Leave No One Behind, as we know, is the universal Warrior Ethos and a pillar of the oaths we took when volunteering to defend our country: *we shall never leave a fallen comrade.* As a veteran in long-term recovery, I embrace a similar commitment to always be there for those who seek the fellowship of recovery. This anthology keeps me connected to both oaths and both communities.

As I read the entries—which span all services, Canadian and American—I feel strength, hope, and solidarity. They put me in a positive, healthy mind-space. I wish I'd had a resource like this when I was battling addiction and simultaneously trying to serve my country—serving two masters, if you will. The stigma was real, and shame clouded my thoughts. Addiction felt like weakness and failure, especially in an environment where we were expected to be the "best of the best." I felt alone. *Leave No One Behind* is a daily reminder that we are not alone. A reminder that not only do we share common experiences around drinking, trauma, abuse, and stigma but also camaraderie, service, sacrifice, and survival.

Each entry is a deeply personal celebration of recovery, life, and freedom and an act of giving back. A symbol of triumph, victory, and gratitude. By sharing these powerful messages through our personal stories, we reduce stigma, help each other heal, and provide fuel for our sober lives so we are healthy enough to help the next veteran, neighbor, loved one, or friend.

I am grateful to all of my fellow veterans who contributed to this powerful anthology and to each of you finding it along your journey. While we may have served, experienced addiction, and found recovery at different times, in different places, and with different people, *Leave No One Behind* unites us once again as an intimately connected community and family. Each day's reading is like an extended hand, one veteran to the next. I hope you feel that too, and that this becomes a treasure you turn to again and again—not just for the words, but for the spirit of one another.

Alta D., U.S. Navy 1991–2016
Alta DeRoo, MD, Chief Medical Officer, Hazelden Betty Ford Foundation

JANUARY

Stigma

There is a massive stigma for those of us who continued drinking in civilian life the way we did in the service.

People think, *There's that old drunk again. Now he's in jail; let's dry him up. He's not much good. He may have been, but he's no good for anything now. All those nice ribbons represented something, but he's nothing anymore.* They just laugh at you. That's all you are: a joke. That's hard to live with. Yeah.

But we drinkers just think, *If only I had someone to watch my back again.*

The thing is, we just need someone who understands—who can share our experience as someone who is a veteran and who has experienced addiction. When we start to connect with each other, the stigma dissolves, and we realize we are not unique. That means we can do this thing—if we stick together.

Today I'll reject the stigma of recovery and remember that I can do this if I stick with others.

—Dan N., U.S. Army, 1971–1977

A Fellowship of Suffering

One of the things I like about AA is that they are people who have been marginalized. I get that.

It's a fellowship of suffering. I get that. If you hang in together, you a chance to get through this thing.

Soldiers fight not for the hatred of the enemy in front of them, but for the love of the men behind them. Medals awarded almost always include caring for others while at peril for their own safety.

It's the same thing with recovery.

I will fight just as hard for myself as for the suffering person beside me. I will leave no one behind.

—Don E., U.S. Army, 1967–1970

Alcoholism and Separating
from the Air Force

When I separated from the Air Force, I was drinking heavily. It was difficult to transition back to civilian life after being in the military. It's such a difficult transition that you can't prepare for this change. All of a sudden, you're a civilian again. The camaraderie you had in the Air Force, the community and all the resources, are suddenly gone, and you're just home. Instead of that community, now you're back with people who don't understand what you went through while you were in the Air Force—especially your spouse. I had a lot of inner conflict with this. On top of that, I was trying to reconnect with my children. I felt like I had lost a few years with them, and it felt bad.

To be honest, I was just lost. I drank to manage that level of stress and isolation. The isolation fueled my alcoholism. I didn't know how to make this transition on my own. But eventually, I got help.

I got help by connecting with others in recovery. They helped me feel like there were other ways to cope with transitions in life—that I'm not alone.

Today I will connect with others when I feel
stressed or isolated.

—Anonymous, U.S. Air Force, 1997–2000

You Owe It to Yourself

You have done what countless millions have not or would not do. Under the direst of conditions, you have proven that you have what it takes to complete the mission. And now, as you continue the process, remember to include yourself. First and foremost, include yourself.

As your journey continues, put yourself up front. Give reality to the ghosts of your past. Once that's done, stop trying to alter your past. Don't regret your past, but don't shut the door on it. It is what it is. It should be a life lesson, not a life sentence. Manifest your best future. An infinite amount of possible futures wait for you to decide which one will be reality for you. Only you can decide which one.

Just for today, for this moment, at this time,
I will put myself first.

—Ed C., U.S. Army, 1975–1979

Willing to Do ANYTHING
to Support My Recovery

When I was using, I became willing to do anything to get the next one. I spent years of my life trying to kill myself for things I had already survived. Trauma had become my master. Getting high was my only coping skill, and even that had lost its effect. I will never forget when the therapist from the VA asked me if I was willing to try and get help. I was scared, but I had nothing left to lose. I had just enough willingness to take her advice and get some help. When I saw my life starting to slowly get better, there was a turning point. I became willing to do whatever it took to become the person I was meant be.

Before the trauma and before the drugs, I always felt I was meant to do something great. Now that I have put some time together, I see the value in practicing recovery principles in every area of my life. When I became willing, I started down my path to greatness.

*Today I will allow the seed of willingness to take root
in my life. For my recovery to blossom, I must practice
recovery principles in every area of my life.*

—Emil C., U.S. Navy, 1995–1997

Culture Change / Change of Culture

There was a no-alcohol rule in Iraq. I thought, *I'm twenty. I'm in the military. I'm in a combat zone. Why can't I drink?* But buying into everything my supervisors said, I mentally and physically went with the flow and culture around me. I embraced my work and didn't deal with anything. I pushed my issues off to the side and stayed committed to the mission.

Then I returned home. It wasn't a combat situation, and alcohol was everywhere. I was left with myself to deal with what and how I wanted.

After my last big drinking binge, I reached out for help and discovered a different way of life—a different culture with the same rule: no alcohol.

Today recovery is an extension of my personal culture and commitment.

—Anonymous, U.S. Army, 2005–2009

Rebuilding Bridges

It's taken me a long time to build up the bridges that I burned and to find my way back. I'm still learning. I have a hard time talking about it, because I'm not used to sharing this kind of stuff with others, particularly people who haven't been through it. But I know that this stuff is poison, and I need to tell my story. Somebody needs to hear this.

When I decided that I was ready to get this shit out of me, the first doctor I talked to was a resident. I started talking and her eyes looked so big and she looked like a deer in the headlights. Then she stopped me in the middle of my sentence and said, "I think we need somebody that's a little more qualified to handle this to talk to you." She didn't react that way out of malice. I've been through some serious shit, and it's heavy. I understand what she was trying to do, that she was trying to do the right thing, but what that response did in my mind was prove to me that I am the monster that I believed myself to be.

So I just clammed up, because it's hard to explain my experience to somebody that's never been through any of it. I didn't talk about it again until a few years back. Now I know that keeping the poison bottled up twisted how I saw myself.

I will find people who understand where I've been
. . . and I will be that person for someone else.

—Bradley L., U.S. Army, 2005–2010

Scars Heal

My friend and I were at an all-night eating establishment, and I got hammered. After I said some off-color remarks to somebody who yelled at my friend, I got jumped. They picked me up and put my face directly on the ground. I was charged with drunk and disorderly, and spent the night in jail.

Just over a week later, I fell asleep in my car in front of a gas station—the car was still running. I got a DUI.

Really, I should've gotten plenty more. Later, I wrecked a car. Things started to pile up; relationships changed. Friends went away.

In the past, I had backed out of an enlistment, so I decided to talk to those fine people at the Navy recruiting office again. I had my degree and wanted to explore options for getting an officer commission. I was told it would take a couple months to get me in. I knew that in another couple of months, I was going to get in a hell of a lot more trouble. So, I enlisted. Boot camp was amazing. It took the liquor away and put a little rigor in my life.

Over thirteen years later, I'm a sober naval officer with a small, visible reminder of my life before—a scar on my forehead from the night my face was on the ground.

May our scars serve as visible reminders
of our journey in recovery.

—Matthew S., U.S. Navy, 2006–Currently Serving

Remove the Mask

I was the poster child for the Army. In life in general, I always gave 100 percent effort. I never drank during the week. On the weekend, I let loose. I lived for the weekend. Monday came, and I would shake the cobwebs off and do morning PT.

I was very good at masking my life. If you were to look at me, there's no way you'd believe this guy had issues. I was a performer, an overachiever. But don't be fooled. I lied a lot. I lied, in my mind, for good reasons. I didn't want to disappoint. I wasn't trying to hurt people with my lies. My performance was a cover-up for ongoing issues.

As I walk my new journey in sobriety, I am learning I no longer have to perform.

In recovery, I can present myself to the world without hesitation, hindrance, or regret.

—Kory W., Canadian Armed Forces, 2009–2015

Community in the Army and in Recovery

I joined the Army when I was seventeen years old. My first duty station was Berlin. If you ever think about what a POW camp looks like, that was Berlin, because we were surrounded by a wall and about 200,000 East German soldiers.

The bonds that I had with the people in my platoon were a huge part of my active-duty experience. These are the guys that you bled with, you sweated with, you trained with. You entrusted your life to these guys.

When I left active duty, I came back to the States and went to college. I immediately felt out of place. I was surrounded by other students who hadn't been deployed. I felt lost. I started drinking to try to feel normal.

But in recovery, I have found that solidarity again. The bonds that I have with my veteran community are amazing. We can talk about our time in the military and our time on the streets, because we've had the same experiences. It's almost like a family. These people are a key component of my recovery.

Today I will seek out connection,
because it is the opposite of addiction.

—JR W., U.S. Army, 1987–1995

Leave No One Behind

In the military, you hear, "Leave no one behind." But the reality is, we get left behind all the time. Especially women.

I was left behind. I was left behind by poor leadership. I was left behind by female NCOs, and I was left behind by my command. I think this plays a huge role in how women feel when they get out of the military.

Even as an employee of the VA now, I've often closed myself off to female veterans, so I've had to work really hard to open myself up and connect with them. Now that I have, I've made some incredible relationships. The women are amazing. I wasn't taught that as a woman in the military, so I know it's hard for women vets to get support. But there are so many resources out there for women who are having difficulty getting back in the world.

Since I opened myself up to women veterans—especially the older ones—I've learned so much and gotten so much compassion in return.

Today I am committed to leaving no woman
veteran behind. Today I will offer a helping hand,
a listening ear, compassion, and support.

—Berlynn F., U.S. Marine Corps, 2009–2011

I Didn't Trust Myself

When I was drinking, I didn't trust anyone. But what I've learned is, the root of that distrust was my lack of trust in myself.

I didn't trust anybody, because I didn't trust myself. I couldn't trust myself to stay sober, and I couldn't trust myself to stay out of trouble. Essentially, my life was unmanageable, so I wasn't about to trust somebody else!

But once I got into the veteran program and met these other veterans and developed a sense of trust and loyalty with them . . . that really helped me come to terms with what trust means and reminded me of the lack of trust I was dealing with in myself.

> *On this day, I will think about trust and the importance of a sobriety circle.*

—Mike D., U.S. Marine Corps, 1970–1974

Putting Pen to Paper

There are very few material things I need in this world, but I cannot be without pen and paper.

I speak only in meetings, so writing has always been a gateway for me to learn how to communicate my thoughts and feelings. It's been an integral part of my sobriety. I have journals from fourteen years ago that I still hold on to. They chart my evolution.

For me, writing is a form of meditation and prayer. Sometimes I write "Dear God" letters, and just go on and on. There are times I've even cussed God out—like, *What the fuck is going on, God?* That's the type of relationship I have with him.

If I'm feeling jacked up or off or something is bothering me, it's a sign I need to put pen to paper. It's a way of getting it all out. I pour everything inside me onto the page. It's like the feeling I have after I take a bubble bath; all those emotions go down the drain.

Today I will chart my course by putting pen to paper, using writing as release. I'll use writing as a prayer.

—Elora K., U.S. Navy, 1997–2007

New Routine

I think we all still have a little manipulation left in us, no matter where we're at in sobriety. The Navy highly recommended I attend meetings, and I had to go get that stupid paper signed. I picked the treatment center director's wife to be my sponsor, because I thought it would look good on my record. They would be at the meetings, but I didn't know they didn't keep a record of my attendance. I honestly thought there was some chart or whatever.

Well, the thing is, they adopted me and treated me like a daughter. My first sponsor even coached me through labor with my oldest son. We developed such a close bond that, as the years went by, people new to the area thought my sponsor and her husband were my parents.

They spoiled me. They fed me. They picked me up and we'd go to their miniature farm. They'd have barbecues, meetings, and Easter egg hunts there. I told myself, *Let's just try this on for size, because what's happening now is way better than what was happening. I can deal with this.*

As I travel the road of recovery, I willingly welcome new people and new horizons into my life.

—Mary H., U.S. Navy, 1984–2004

Becoming Myself

Long-distance running used to be my first "drug of choice," until drinking took over. I started drinking before basic, but I really drank a lot when I was stationed in Germany, because Germany was all about drinking.

I grew up with an alcoholic father who was constantly getting admitted to the hospital and psych units. I didn't want my drinking to progress to that point. I knew if I didn't get sober, I was gonna die. I had tried to stop drinking. I went to Al-Anon, but I never worked the Steps. I'd get drunk, and they said maybe I needed a different program. I tried therapy, but the therapist said she couldn't help me until I stopped drinking.

I didn't get sober until after active duty, when I joined the National Guard. There was a girl in my Guard unit who helped me find some AA meetings. I started going to meetings all the time.

I had friends in my Guard unit who didn't even realize I had a problem, because they were so used to seeing me drinking all the time. When I got sober, they were like, "Holy Moly, you're totally different!"

Today I am grateful that recovery has allowed me to become who I was meant to be.

—Deb L., U.S. Army, 1981–1996

High Expectations

I thought I could erase what happened in the past.

I had really built myself up for this career as a Navy man, because it was a family thing. It's what I wanted to do, but more importantly, it's what I thought would make my father and my family happy. I spent a lot of time preparing for the Navy, including ROTC. Seventeen years old and a signed waiver was all I needed for a new beginning and permission to conquer the world.

In my mind, joining the Navy just like my father and grandfather was a rite of passage. I had high expectations of what life was going to be like when I got into the military. All those expectations came crashing down when I was sexually assaulted in boot camp. I want to say it strengthened me or made me a better or a more resilient person, but it didn't. I struggled to maintain sobriety after the assault and trauma. I spent a lot of time just trying to erase what happened to me.

Many years later, I decided to reconcile my past with the military and get some help for the military sexual trauma using EMDR therapy. Having my trauma acknowledged didn't erase it, but it helped me develop an identity for myself. I know who I am today.

The impact of trauma can be subtle, insidious, and even outright destructive. True acknowledgment is necessary for my healing to begin.

—Emil C., U.S. Navy, 1995–1997

Hitting Bottom

I was a heavy drug and alcohol user before I went into the Navy. I wasn't allowed to use drugs in the service, but I drank all the harder in the military. For my first duty, I was stationed on a minesweeper in Bahrain for about a year. I went out and drank whenever I could. When I came back stateside, I did more of the same.

After I got out of the military, I added drugs back into the mix. It wasn't until last year that I really started to work on recovery. I had an episode where I was committed to the psychiatric ward at the local VA hospital, and that was due to heavy drug and alcohol use. After that, I've been in group meetings. Through the VA and weekly therapy, I've been trying to get through drug and alcohol issues. Now I am in recovery trying to live a better life.

I will say that going through that terrible hospital episode has helped me pursue sobriety. Sometimes hitting bottom can bring on the change that's needed to make different choices.

Hitting bottom is painful, but today I will remember that it can motivate us to make a change.

—John K., U.S. Navy, 2005–2009

How the Military Helps with Tools of Sobriety

I got sober before I joined the military. I'd already been doing recovery work for seven years by the time I joined.

In basic training, they're going to get your ass out of bed at four o'clock, they're going to make sure that your uniform is spit-and-polish, and they're going to make sure that you know where to go and what time in what uniform.

Really all that is doing is just preparing somebody for life. Those are just simple life lessons that you're going to carry with you: suit up and show up, be punctual, and be there in the right uniform.

These are important lessons in the military. But they're also important lessons in life that new recruits probably don't know and aren't motivated to learn. So the military puts all these kinds of external motivations to do that.

In a lot of ways, I already had that external motivation from my time in recovery. I knew that in order to stay sober, there were things that I had to do and things I had to avoid. The military reinforced those lessons for me.

Today I will use the tools of sobriety. I will suit up and show up and keep my obligations.

—J. D., U.S. Army, 1985–1993/1998–2018

Addiction Is Cunning, Baffling, and Powerful

I never said no to anything in the service, but alcohol was my primary drug of choice. I got deployed to Afghanistan in 2002. That's when my serious drinking started.

When we got there, there was nothing—no running water, no electricity—same conditions as in a combat zone. But there was still booze. It's really hot in the Middle East, so we worked at night and slept during the day. That was a hard adjustment for many of us, so we started sneaking alcohol in. A lot of us drank almost daily to take the edge off. Then we'd just pass out. I didn't realize it at the time, but something had changed. After several deployments, I started to feel invincible. There was a thrill to living on the edge. And alcohol was a big part of that.

But we weren't invincible.

I will never forget what I learned in recovery: Addiction is cunning, baffling, and powerful. It sneaks up on you, then takes over your life.

All of this is why admitting our powerlessness
is the First Step.

—Kenneth B., U.S. Air Force, 2001–2007

Who's Truly at Fault?

For so many years, I felt as though the Army had betrayed me. I now have a different opinion. I now feel as though it's not the Army's fault, nor is it the Army's responsibility, what I went through. Because I'm definitely an alcoholic. In other circles, I identify as an addict. I come from a very long line of addicts and alcoholics on both sides.

But this change in perspective is a gift from the sobriety program I'm a part of. Because for so many years, I did blame the Army. I've made a hell of a victim and a hell of a martyr. Like, let me be the one to take those bad experiences and turn them into a horrible excuse to completely destroy my life.

Because now, the same God that I used to wonder, *Where the fuck were you when I needed you most?* I now can look back and see those hard times, just like footprints in the sand. Those weren't times I was alone. Those were times he carried my sorry ass.

Today I will examine areas where I feel like a martyr and take responsibility where I need to.

—Jenna R., U.S. Army, 2005–Currently Serving

Demons and Redemption

When I came home, I battled my demons for two years. The pills led to heroin and then wreckage.

I had been looking for absolution for all the things that I had done. But how could I ever have absolution when there were questions that would never be answered? So, instead, I found acceptance. I accepted what I had to become in order to survive. I finally understood that I became a monster in those moments, because monsters are what those moments required. Monsters got the job done.

But a monster is not truly who I am. Monsters don't feel the remorse that I feel. Monsters don't long for it to have gone any other way than the way it did. Monsters don't ache for redemption. But I do.

Today I work with the most vulnerable veteran demographic, those battling addiction. They aren't monsters either. They're battling their demons like I did. I go to prisons. I go out under bridges. I go to needle exchanges. I go where others won't go, because I've been right where my brothers and sisters are now. My goal is to be the person that I needed all those years ago that I couldn't seem to find. I want to give back without giving them a reason to give up.

Today I will remember that there can be peace in survival.

—Bradley L., U.S. Army, 2005–2010

Fear Factor

For me, the motivating factor for not telling people I was in recovery was fear. I didn't know what that was going to be like. I was always afraid, not only about how I was going to be perceived but also of whether it would be held against me. Would it limit me? Would I be different?

So I never let my superiors know, because I wasn't going to give them an opportunity to treat me differently. I'm not saying they would, but that was my way of protecting myself from the unknown.

Sometimes I met with people outside of my command. One such person was a Navy counselor on a ship; we would meet for lunch. The neat thing was—he was in recovery. Talking to somebody like me was a lot easier than somebody who's judging me based on my education or training. Who better to go see on the other side of the desk?

*Today I will have a spirit of discernment
when sharing my recovery with others.*

—Joe II., U.S. Navy, 1988–2015

Therapy

Going to seek therapy is not seen as the most macho thing to do. The thinking is, *I should be able to take care of these issues myself.*

There were a few reasons I was hesitant to go to therapy in recovery. For one, I had done therapy growing up and I felt like it never helped me—actually, I felt like it made things worse. For another, I tried to see a therapist a couple times when I was in the military for my mental health, and both times it was a negative experience where this guy looked at me and literally called me a loser and told me that I was wasting his time.

But in recovery, I have found therapy to be helpful. Nowadays I see my therapist about once a month, where it used to be weekly. I think there was a period where we talked almost every day, and now I only talk to her like once a month as I need to.

*Today I will recognize that therapy can be used
as one of the tools of recovery.*

—Dennis D., U.S. Army, 1997–2003

Even Sailors Can Be Drunks

I'm Bud, and I'm an alcoholic. I've been sober forty-two years, but when I say sober, I mean sometimes I'm dry and sometimes I'm sober. When I'm sober, I'm at peace, happy, joyous, and free. When I'm dry, I'm too much in my head, ranting and raving.

My parents didn't really drink much, and I only drank a little in high school, because I was afraid they'd catch me. I joined the Navy Reserves in high school and went on active duty after graduation. That's when my drinking really took off. I left for my first deployment to the western Pacific in 1959, nine hours after I married my high school sweetheart.

I had an alcohol problem from day one. In Hong Kong, I hocked my high school ring that my parents got me so I could buy booze. And I remember coming back after drinking with buddies. The closer we got to the ship, the drunker we acted. They called us gangway drunks.

I bragged about how much I could drink, until something clicked and I started feeling guilty. Then this guy said, "Hell, son, you're not a drunk. You're just a sailor." It was just the excuse I needed.

Today I'm grateful that in recovery we seek guidance, rather than offer excuses.

—Bud N., U.S. Navy, 1957–1983

Drinking in the Military

Drinking was just a way of life in the military, and everyone was doing it. At night in the barracks, everyone was expected to be drinking and hanging out. So it was just all normal life.

Not only that, if you weren't drinking, people would look at you funny, and they didn't know what to expect of you next. I went along with that pressure, because it was easier—plus I liked to drink. But alcohol definitely made things harder. With PT in the morning, my hangovers would keep me underhydrated and mentally scattered. Afternoons were okay, because by that point, I was sobering up.

But at night, I would just drink again and keep the cycle going. When I got out of the military, the drinking didn't stop. I showed up to work still reeking of booze, only now this behavior wasn't seen as normal. Thankfully, my boss was a veteran too, and he gave me a second chance. He said, "You're a good employee, and I know it's hard getting out of service, but you need to get some help." He gave me the number to the VA office, and I've been on this journey ever since.

*Today I will be grateful that I was able
to stop the cycle of addiction.*

—Eric S., U.S. Marine Corps, 2005–2009

Letting Go and Trusting God

My treatment counselors had seen people like me before, and they suggested I see someone for my military issues. They made an appointment for me at the local veteran center. In July 1993, just six weeks sober, I went. On the walls were some memorabilia—pictures of military things.

By the time I got in to see the counselor, all these emotions were pretty close to the surface. He asked me to describe a couple of events I found troubling. When I did, I noticed he was crying. He happened to be a Vietnam vet who had twelve years of sobriety. By the time I ended my session, I had what he called a flooding experience. Everything stuffed deep down inside came back all at once. I was terrified, and more than anything I wanted another drink.

What I did instead, I stopped at the local Vietnam memorial on my way home. I got down on my knees and asked God for help. I decided to turn my will over to a God I had abandoned twenty-five years ago. And I didn't realize it immediately, but the compulsion to flee to alcohol and drugs was gone.

Even though I was sober, it took turning my will over to God for me to finally stop the automatic urge to drink or use drugs.

—Doc D., U.S. Army, 1968–1970

Sponsorship Saves

For years, I used to think that acceptance meant I had to like something to accept it.

Oh, no, I don't have to like it. I just need to accept it. To let it go. There's a lot of things I don't like about my life, but today is like, wow.

One of the amazing things I've learned in recovery is how to be somebody's sponsor. I have AA pamphlets and the sponsorship book. As your sponsor, I'm not willing to let you just flop around and not do something. I'm not going to let you waste your time; we're going to work together. That's something else I tell my sponsees: if you don't make progress with me, I will cut you loose so you can find the one that's supposed to be working with you.

Today I'll remember that working with others through mentorship and sponsorship brings progress on my path of recovery.

—Stephanie C., U.S. Navy, 1978–1983

It Was the Norm

In the Army, I spent a long sixteen months in Iraq with the unit. It was hot—140 degrees in the shade—and sometimes below freezing at night. Iraq was something that I wasn't used to; it was different. It was also scary, because we were right in the middle of everything. We were looking for the bad guys—most of the time doing route clearance looking for IEDs and EFPs—anyone setting up those devices, all hours of the day. It was crazy.

After my deployments in Iraq, I found myself struggling with more than I brought with me into the military. There was so much that happened. Some people drank in the barracks in garrison and some, like me, ran the streets of Fayetteville. Within a week of our unit's return, we had one fatal crash due to a DWI, two suicides on base, and family violence. There was just a slew of turmoil, dilemma, pain, and suffering that came back with us. It was the norm.

We went through it all together as a unit. We kept quiet about it. We didn't speak about it.

My addiction keeps me quiet. Sobriety serves as a loudspeaker. My sobriety helps me overcome the struggles, suffering, and discomforts of my past.

—Armando S., U.S. Army, 2006–2009

Stay for Yourself

I had two sons. One was born in August of 1989 and the other in February of 1991. My disease had progressed so much that I was still using, even though I had my children. They didn't have a mother during that time. They were with me, but I wasn't with them. I was putting the drugs before my children. It finally got to the point where I wasn't with my family at all. When my kids were no longer staying with me, I told myself that I need to do something different now.

Until that point, I hadn't heard about the VA. When I got out of the U.S. Air National Guard in '91, I never went. While I was using, my world was small. Another addict told me about the VA and the programs it offered. I got in contact with a representative and told her, "I need to get my life together."

My reason for going in was initially for my kids—to get them back. I'm glad that I went in for them, but I stayed for myself. Sometimes when you go into recovery it can be for one thing, but you got to stay for yourself. Anything can get you in there; only you can keep you there.

The reason for you to stay in recovery is for you. If you don't stay for yourself, you're not going to stay.

—Karen A., U.S. Air National Guard, 1980–1991

One More Day

While serving in the Army, I did all kinds of stuff in Germany. I went to go visit somebody I knew from the base before and ended up learning all about the goodies that came from Turkey, if you know what I mean.

I ended up finding out about stuff I could make money on and had gotten some connections where I was stationed. It didn't last after I got back to the States, so it was easy for me to give it up. But alcohol was my main drug of choice throughout, I was well known for my ability to drink anybody under the table.

Nobody expected me to get sober. Thirty-seven years later, I'm still celebrating my sobriety.

No matter what others think of my journey, today I look forward to celebrating one more day of sobriety— one more day of celebrating myself.

—Gayle C., U.S. Army National Guard, 1976–1980/1984

God Keeps Giving

I am grateful for the gifts of recovery. Obviously, I have to put in work toward this program. And I'm okay with doing it every day—for the rest of my life. I used every day—I also put a lot of work into that. But today I have these little changes in my life. I want to put the work into my recovery.

Looking back, I have so much more in my life today than I ever had before. I'm not talking about materialistic things; I'm talking about spiritual ones. From the glow in my eyes to the fire in my heart.

You can't put a monetary value on the life I have today. It's worth so much more than anything I've ever gotten.

God keeps giving and giving and giving.

—John F., U.S. Air Force, 1985–1996

FEBRUARY

Drinking Culture, and No Sick Days

While I was never explicitly pressured to drink in the Air Force, I easily fell into the habit. We'd celebrate in the officers club, and we'd drink together on weekends. It's how we socialized and let off steam.

One morning I was so sick from drinking over the weekend that I called in sick. But I was told, "You can't call out in the military. Come to the emergency room, and we'll tell you whether or not you can be out sick." When I got to the ER they gave me IV fluids, they gave me nausea medicine, and they sent me right to my floor to take care of patients. No one pointed out that I surely smelled like alcohol. No one told me this was abnormal. It was like they were condoning my drinking.

It took a while, but once I got out of the military, I realized that I can make different choices. I don't have to get sick from alcohol. In fact, I never have to drink again.

*Today I will be grateful for the opportunity
to live a sober life.*

—Anonymous, U.S. Air Force, 1997–2000

A New Way of Life

From the age of nine through my time in the military, I struggled with active addiction. My addiction started as a direct result of my environment—my family. My parents sold narcotics, and my mother and siblings were and are addicts. When I was in the military, we always were able to use some type of substance. My active addiction ultimately led to me leaving the military early, with eleven years, thankfully with an honorable discharge.

After leaving, my life was in a steady decline until I finally reached out to a mental health and addictions VA program for help. This was God doing for me what I could not do for myself. Then I left there, got my two sons back, went to school, got a job, found a place to live, and am happily married. Our adult sons are grown, own homes, and have fabulous jobs. Now I'm retired, and we are about to adopt two boys.

I have a sponsor, I work the Steps, I do service, and I sponsor others. I give back what is so freely given to me.

Today I will pray, read a meditation, read my Bible,
and thank my Higher Power for the blessings
of this new way of life!

—Karen A., U.S. Air Force, 1980–1991

The Next Right Thing

You survived insufferable torment in your service. Find grace in knowing that you were placed in extraordinary circumstances that asked of you unimaginable deeds. Find peace in your certainty that you did all that was asked of you and more. You showed uncommon bravery and fortitude. Today, of course, you question some of the decisions you made. Rest easy in the knowledge that you always did the right thing in the moment. It wasn't fair and it wasn't pretty. But you and your men came home.

You led them through a hell no one should ever have to experience. Even in the final moments of some of your brothers, you saw that they went out with peace in their eyes even as the world burned around them. Your presence gave them the comfort and courage to proceed into that hereafter without fear in their gazes.

Addiction brought with it its own kind of hell. Now we look to those on either side of us, and we lead them through it. We show it can be done. We do the next right thing as we work our program. We give back to others. We give our presence and service to them so they can find peace too. So they can find their way through the fire.

Today I will look for the grace in my past,
my present, and my future.

—Bradley L., U.S. Army, 2005–2010

He Asked the Question

Early in my enlistment, I went to a disciplinary review board, where we pop tall in front of a bunch of senior enlisted guys who have been around a long time. I heard there would be a lot of yelling and getting my ass chewed. Instead they tried to figure out what was going on and determine the level of disciplinary action I needed.

In the back of the room, a senior chief asked, "Do you think you might be an alcoholic?" The air completely sucked out of the room. I didn't know what it meant entirely and had never had somebody in a position of authority that I trusted ask me that question before.

I didn't have a lot of people I trusted in life; I still don't have a lot of people I trust in life, but I trusted the wisdom in that room. The seed of recovery was planted when he asked the question.

Day by day, open-mindedness fertilizes
the seed of my recovery.

—Matthew S., U.S. Navy, 2006–Currently Serving

Slowly Ease the Pain

Each and every day I ask, *What do I have? What have I been left with? What can I do with what I have? Who was I then? Who am I now? What can I do with who I am now? Where did I end up? What can I do with where I ended up? How can I accomplish success in small increments? How can I do more in life? What more can I do in life?*

I can keep asking questions. Look for answers. Make plans with the answers. Pray a lot. Try to keep calm and clear. Learn meditation. Learn how to react to the people around me with smoother responses. Remind myself that I am eternally sanding down the rough edges. Be thankful I got to see and live through another day.

My disability limits me. My disability creates a new life that I can explore. I can have full life. Life, liberty, and the pursuits of happiness are possible. My job is to understand my past and keep on the path of life. My life is like an ongoing patrol. My never-ending mission. I accept this.

Today I will learn to love and appreciate those around me and what we can do together.

—Moe A., U.S. Marine Corps, 1962–1966

Keeping It Simple

I loved my military service and was deployed a couple times and got to see so much. When 9/11 happened, I was in Germany and got attached to an Apache unit to go into Kuwait. I came back to the States, got attached to a unit already in Iraq, and was sent back a few months later.

My unit included all NCOs and upper NCOs. It wasn't a normal unit or schedule where we had PT at 0630. With a lot of downtime and nice weather, we'd barbecue and drink in the barracks.

After almost nine years of active duty, I did the rest of my time in the Reserves, working one weekend a month. It was because of this decision that a smooth transition to becoming a civilian was possible. For me, it helped being away from full-time military service to stay on the recovery path.

I've adjusted, and I'm thankful. Now I assemble parts for a large company. I'm not an office person, and there isn't a big drinking culture after work. I punch in, clock out, and attend meetings.

A simple transition makes for a grand entrance.

—Jen O., U.S. Army, 1995–2019

Getting Rid of My Crutch

When I came home from the Marines, alcohol was my crutch to deal with the world. I was denying that my service affected me negatively. I continued to lean on my crutch more and more. I knew I needed something to help me, but I did not know what I needed.

Years later, when my PTSD came to a head, I acknowledged the mental wounds I left the military with. Being in the Middle East changed me. I saw things that I can never unsee.

However, with the help of other veterans, exercise, therapy, medicines, and meditation, I am living my best life without alcohol. I accept that I will never be the person I was before I joined the Marine Corps, but I no longer depend on alcohol to help me survive each day.

*Today I will be grateful for my service and
will work to stand tall without crutches.*

—Eric S., U.S. Marine Corps, 2005–2009

A Brotherhood for the Better

I got hurt in the Army. Because of my injury I went from being a part of an immediate response unit to working as a desk person. I took to it poorly. I didn't want to be in the background.

I didn't like feeling down, shitty, and out with alcohol. I liked being up—*go, go, go*—and cocaine became my drug of choice. At first it was introductory, only on the weekends. I felt like I didn't need to sleep for three days.

There were a lot of people around me who were laying down the law and the rules, and they were using too. So I kind of had free rein. It was an "I know you know, but no one knows" thing, and that made for an awkward work environment. It was like, *I was just doing cocaine with you for two days, and now you're yelling at me because my boots aren't polished. What the hell is that?* I didn't like that in myself either. I was doing the same to my subordinates.

It was a brotherhood for the worse—controversial, contradicting, and fake.

Today I have a brotherhood and sisterhood for the better.

—Kory W., Canadian Armed Forces, 2009–2015

Substances and Service Both Change Our Perceptions

Addiction tricks you into believing that everything's okay. Meanwhile, your life is deteriorating right in front of you. You want to blame everything but the alcohol. Sometimes our lives have to get to a point where the damage is clear before we can see the changes we need to make to get clean.

Our experiences as veterans don't always help. A lot of us have considerable baggage from when we were deployed. We just want to feel normal, but instead we feel out of place and numb. A lot of us develop PTSD.

Not only do substances change the way we think, but a lot of us keep our own personal hurt lockers and don't get the help we need to find perspective and heal.

I work in the VA hospital that helped me get sober. I just celebrated my fourth year of sobriety. I help others follow the same path that I did, and I think we give each other hope—that we can get help, and that our perceptions aren't permanently damaged.

Today I will be open to changing my
perceptions, and heal.

—JR W., U.S. Army, 1987–1995

Building a Framework for Recovery

As I've changed, so has my support system. It's about what and who is helping me grow. I didn't use around my family members, so they didn't see the destruction of my addiction. I'd get high and leave. Just disappear. So I'm rebuilding a lot of those relationships.

I'm a veteran, and I work at the VA now. I tell the vets I work with that recovery is like laying bricks. We create a foundation on which we build straight walls of recovery. We build that foundation with people and support. But, just as with bricks, sometimes relationships crack and break, and you have to either get rid of them or mend them.

If people aren't helping you build your network of recovery, it might be time to move on or reconstruct a healthier relationship.

Today I will strengthen those relationships that build upon my solid foundation of recovery and growth.

—Berlynn F., U.S. Marine Corps, 2009–2011

You Deserve to Treat Yourself Better

As a veteran, you've done what countless millions of other people cannot or will not do, and that is serve this country. And you deserve the best. You deserve to treat yourself better. You deserve to allow people to treat you better.

To get that, you need to give 110 percent every day. I don't want to have to use a phrase from the Army, but you do need to "be the best you can be."

I would encourage you most desperately to take care of yourself. Make the effort.

Just for today, I will put the effort in to take care of myself, because I matter.

—Ed C., U.S. Army, 1975–1979

Things I've Learned along the Way

Some things I've learned on my path of recovery:

- There's no shame in crying. I cried through my whole first year of sobriety!
- It doesn't matter if you come from Yale or jail. In AA, the common denominator is alcohol. We're all just trying to get and stay sober.
- In recovery, you get to choose your family.
- Recovery is about more than staying sober. In my opinion, going "cold turkey" on your own is just a dry drunk.
- Sobriety means we feel again, which can be hard. But we need to feel it before we can heal it.
- You might not get the help you need from the military. The important thing is to get help. And if you can't find a group or meeting that fits you, find and participate in a recovery program online.
- Service work is the foundation of recovery. You help yourself when you help others.
- Use *Let go and let God / Let go and let God / Let go and let God* as your new cadence.

Today I know that recovery takes time and practice. Each day is a new beginning, with a new lesson and a new gift.

—Elora K., U.S. Navy, 1997–2007

I Choose Sobriety

At sixteen months dry, I relapsed, and the squadron sent me to the galley for temporary additional duty. It was there that I met my first husband. He relapsed. I relapsed. We got married. I ended up getting pregnant again.

He went out for a short thirty-day deployment. I knew that if I didn't start going back to AA before he came back home, I probably wasn't going to ever get back into it. I went to a meeting. My husband was due to get back the next morning. I picked him up from the boat, and I was like, "Look, this is what's happening. I'm back in recovery."

He was not interested in any way, shape, or form. We stayed together, technically, for maybe a year after that—but it just was not working. Today my sobriety date is still November 23, 1986.

Though my relationships may change during my recovery, my sobriety remains my priority.

—Mary H., U.S. Navy, 1984–2004

It Takes a Community

What I discovered about recovery was that there were people willing to help me, support me, and show me how they got sober—how they stayed sober, you know. I was probably a year or two in sobriety, and I was still having nightmares of Vietnam. It got to the point where I would get up around three times during the night and do perimeter checks—check the windows, the door locks, and look outside in the parking lot. I was afraid to go to sleep, because I knew those demons were waiting for me in my dreams.

After working the Steps of recovery, I've got the peace of mind, and I don't have those dreams anymore.

That's the miracle of recovery.

I learned to embrace my demons, face my fears,
quit running from my past—and I haven't had
one of those nightmares in over twenty years.

—Doc D., U.S. Army, 1968–1970

Amazing Things Happen

At seventeen I was deep into my struggle, and deep into alcohol. I had seven DUIs before I turned twenty-one.

I wanted to see what the Navy really had to offer me. I so badly wanted to make the transformation I had heard about from my father and grandfather. The Navy had a zero-tolerance policy for underage drinking. My punishment was forty-five days of confinement. I was busted down in rank and pay, and finally discharged. I just wanted it to be over. I didn't think it could get worse.

In two years of enlistment, I spent most of the time getting in trouble. I spent none of it doing the things that the military was capable of doing—changing people's lives for the better. Despite all that, I have been able to change my life for the better.

Amazing things happen. Like today, I got a letter from my county councilwoman. She wants to meet with me and a local judge so we can discuss plans for people in the county who are suffering in the opioid epidemic. I can't believe this is my life today. I get to go to lunch with a county council member and a judge. It blows my mind. Wow.

I am changing my life for the better.
Starting today, right here, right now.

—Emil C., U.S. Navy, 1995–1997

The Dead-End Road to Addiction

Genetically speaking, I was fucking doomed because of my family history with alcohol. My father was an abusive alcoholic, and I started doing alcohol and other drugs when I was fourteen. I'm also one of the 82,500 Boy Scouts who were sexually abused by a Boy Scout leader, so I had a lot to deal with at that point.

By seventeen, I was drinking to blackout so I wouldn't have to deal with the shame and guilt I carried. In my junior year, I went to Coast Guard boot camp. In my senior year, I did weekend drills. I was still drinking and smoking dope, but somehow I managed not to test positive. I missed so much school I got expelled.

My obligation to the Coast Guard was to finish school, so when they found out I got expelled, I had to get my GED in a hurry in order to stay in the Reserves. By that time, I decided to get the hell out. I got married at city hall, then went across the street to the recruiter and signed up for active duty. I got assigned to a ship in Portsmouth, Virginia, and the party continued until I found my way to recovery.

Step by Step, day by day, I walk with determination on the road to recovery, knowing all too well how the path to addiction is a dead-end journey.

—Joe K., U.S. Coast Guard, 1988–1996

Getting Sober Means Changing Your View

For me, the biggest struggle in quitting drugs is trying to relearn who you are as a person—who you are without drugs and alcohol in the equation. When you're using for a long time, it's almost like you become a drug.

In active addiction, drugs become central to your daily habit and your daily routine. You also think about money in different terms. Day to day, you think about things like, *I have a hundred dollars, which could buy a cart full of groceries, or X amount of this drug.* So getting sober is about changing your view on everything. It means not thinking about your life in terms of drugs anymore.

This opens you up to a totally new way of seeing the world. I'm still learning what that means, because I'm still changing. But it's a positive thing, and I am open to where it takes me.

On this day, I will be open to relearning
who I am and how sobriety is changing me.

—John K., U.S. Navy, 2005–2009

Step Zero

In the Twelve Step program that I'm in, we often talk about Step Zero. Step Zero is awareness that there is a problem. That awareness is huge. This is what Step Zero looks like: *I realize that drinking is killing me. I have got to stop doing this. I'm gonna quit tomorrow.*

Right? This is said by thousands and thousands of alcoholics and addicts every day. The awareness that something is wrong doesn't always result in getting sober. That's why it's Step Zero.

Step One is admitting I can't do this on my own. I need help admitting that I am powerless. But Step Zero is awareness. That awareness is key to recovery.

Today I will remember that Step Zero is an important part of the sobriety process.

—J. D., U.S. Army, 1985–1993/1998–2018

The Price You Pay If You Want to Play

There's no proper way to prepare for going to war. You're over there—Afghanistan, Bagram, Iraq—and it's 24/7 constant fear. No matter where we'd go, to chow hall or wherever, we were getting mortared or rocketed.

So a lot of us used alcohol to cope. Not exactly a healthy coping skill, but it's what was available at the time. After a night of drinking, you'd wake up the next day and try to do your job, but you're still in this drunken haze. A lot of us were doing the same thing. I guess we just figured it was the price we had to pay if we wanted to play.

I just wanted to feel normal, and the only way I could was to get slightly intoxicated. It takes away some of the anxiety. It kind of brings you to the point where you don't care about much of anything. So it changed the experience by letting you escape reality. You'd get a buzz on and just sort of numb out. At the time, I didn't know how dangerous that was.

Today I celebrate my "new normal"—a life free of the bonds of alcohol, in which I can safely feel again.

—Kenneth B., U.S. Air Force, 2001–2007

Pulling Others Off the Battlefield

When I was in the Marine Corps, it was pounded into your head that you never leave a buddy behind; you never leave a fellow Marine behind. You don't give up on them or leave them on their own.

That message has carried through to me my whole life—especially now in AA. Because the addiction fight is like a battlefield. If I see somebody on that battlefield, and I think I can share something from my knowledge or experience that will help them get off that battlefield, I'm gonna do it. Because I've been on that battlefield and other sober people helped pull me off. I owe it to the next guy to help out if I can.

Today I will remember to help others out where I can.

—Mike D., U.S. Marine Corps, 1970–1974

It Only Works If You Work It

I got my first exposure to Alcoholics Anonymous in 1974, when I was active-duty Navy. Apparently I tried to kill my wife when I was in a blackout, and a buddy stopped me. They sent me to sick bay overnight and to an AA meeting the next morning. I went to meetings regularly for the next few months, then they sent me to a Navy hospital in Long Beach, California. But, even after all that, I still wasn't convinced that I was an alcoholic.

For two years, I went to meetings every day. But I never opened the Big Book. I never worked a single Step. I wasn't drinking and I was getting promoted and that was my goal. At the end of those two years, I stopped going to meetings altogether because I was bored to tears.

I continued this "white-knuckle sobriety" for seven years, got the ultimate promotion I wanted, then started drinking again. I learned it's true what they say about the Twelve Step program: it only works if you work it.

I will work and live my program every day with integrity and commitment, because I now know that true recovery involves much more than staying sober.

—Mike F., U.S. Navy, 1959–1965/1972–1990

Alcohol at West Point and in the Army

I picked up my first drink at the Army-Navy game my freshman year at West Point. A Mike's Hard Lemonade and a full bottle of Jack Daniel's later, I was blacked out. I had no memory after that, but I'm told that I was running down the hallways butt-ass naked, swinging a punch into anything that wants to fight, puking my guts out. I woke up the next morning saying, "I can't wait to do that again"—not a normal reaction for most drinkers.

But I drank that way through college until I graduated. I got commissioned in the Army. And, holy shit, now I can drink like I want to, because it's culturally acceptable. Now it's encouraged by my commanders. Now everyone drinks like this. And I don't have to go to school. I get up in the morning and run it off. And I'm good.

Except eventually, it wasn't good. As my drinking got worse, so did the consequences. I broke my back, and I attempted suicide. The misery took me to some bad places. But speaking of miracles, nowadays I am sober from alcohol and drugs. I'm thankful to God every day for that.

Today I will be grateful for the miracle of my sobriety.

—Jenna R., U.S. Army, 2005–Currently Serving

Work the Program

The ship was pretty tough on me being in recovery, and I think that's something unique to the Navy. The problem was meetings were at night, after normal working hours. And on a ship as an air traffic controller, my primary working hours were at night. So that didn't work out very well.

What the ship taught me was pretty simple—I had to work the program, and I couldn't just go to meetings for a solution. I had to separate the meetings and the people from the program.

If I did the program (meaning the Steps)—if I prayed, if I did all the things that I'm supposed to do, I could stay sober.

Day by day, my recovery program entails
a spiritual program.

—Joe H., U.S. Navy, 1988–2015

A Second Chance at Parenting

When I was in active addiction, there were so many times that I just wasn't present for my kids. They're now fifteen and thirteen. I feel like, in some ways, I've been given a second chance to reconnect with them and show them that I don't want to be that person I used to be anymore. I want to be a good father to them. I want to show them that I can be present to give them the attention and love they deserve.

I am not sure my kids understood my recovery early on, but they do seem to appreciate it now. In fact, my daughter came to a meeting with me. She said that she really liked it and thought they were really friendly. She felt it was a good place to be.

Today I will be grateful for second chances in recovery.

—Dennis D., U.S. Army, 1997–2003

Crystal Ball

I make suggestions to my sponsees on a regular basis. If somebody's struggling, I ask them if they've made it to a meeting yet. If they haven't, I recommend they find a meeting. There's no excuse not to get to a meeting. As I understand it, there are Zoom meetings twenty-four hours a day. There's no excuse. I mean, we can make excuses, but that don't make them so.

Whenever sponsees start viewing the future negatively, I ask them to give me back their crystal ball, because it's obviously broken. Then I give them a new one that tells them good things. If your ball is just showing you negative stuff, you've got to give it back, because life gets beautiful.

I find that when my crystal ball gets a little out of alignment, it's because I may have said or done something I feel guilty about. I try to figure out what I've said and done, and correct it. I also try to take it easy on myself. You can't kick me any harder than I can kick me.

As I travel the road of recovery, I will take the necessary steps to ensure I am walking a path of positivity.

—Stephanie C., U.S. Navy, 1978–1983

Just One More, God

I woke up today and asked God to help me stay sober and to give me strength to do his will, just for today. I am a recovered, homeless veteran of a foreign war. I showed up to AA because the doctors would not release me unless I went to an AA meeting. They said I had only two years left to live if I kept drinking. I lost my family, friends, self, and all of my belongings to alcohol, drugs, and PTSD.

God and AA have given me my life back, including most of my relationships and my self-respect. My bills are paid, and I am sober. The best gift has been my new relationship with my Higher Power (God). He has always been there. Tonight I will get on my knees and say thank you for another day sober.

Amen!

Today I can be grateful for not taking a drink
or drug today, and for all of the gifts of sobriety.
One day at a time!

—Tom B., U.S. Navy, 1992–1994

Getting Sober Means Doing the Opposite

I had to totally immerse myself in the recovery community. I have been sober since I was fifteen, and I am grateful that I stumbled across a formula for recovery. The formula was this: put as much energy into my recovery as I did my addiction.

When I was actively using, I was using every day. Therefore, in recovery, I went to a meeting every day.

Before recovery, I had a subscription to the magazine *High Times,* about where to sell dope, where to get dope, and how to grow dope. So in recovery, I canceled that subscription, and I subscribed to *The Grapevine,* which is AA's monthly magazine.

When I was intoxicated every day, I talked to people who were in addiction—drug friends and alcoholics. Now that I got sober, I changed that around—I talked to people who are in recovery. Everything that I did in addiction, I did the polar opposite of in recovery.

Today I will put as much energy into recovery
as I did into my addiction.

—J. D., U.S. Army, 1985–1993/1998–2018

Spreading the Message of Love

I had trust issues and didn't want to go into a room full of people that I didn't know. It took me a long time to be able to join a group and be honest and open. I wasn't ready to speak of my emotions or feelings. In the beginning, not speaking was the easy part.

Today I am a member of a group with a lot of newcomers. I see myself in all of them. Some share. Some don't. Some of them sit there with no light in their eyes. What do I do? I approach them, welcome them, introduce myself, and say "I love you." That's something I would never have done before. Never.

Imagine how different the world would be if a world full of people did that too.

> *Today I will welcome a newcomer as I was*
> *welcomed in the community of recovery—*
> *with uninhibited love.*

—John F., U.S. Air Force, 1985–1996

Coming Home

Because of the skills I got in the Navy, I was able to land a job as an electronics mechanic at a semiconductor plant in Texas. I made a lot of money and thought my life was going to get better. I had three boys, all under kindergarten age. I wanted my husband to support me by taking care of them, but he wanted to remain a truck driver. I paid my mother to watch them.

I had no clue about addiction when my husband was in the grips of it. I just knew it cost me a lot of money. After my first paycheck, I went to the store and my card wouldn't work. Turns out my husband was using our debit card to get money from the ATM, twenty dollars at a time for his habit. He went through my whole check in about twelve hours.

I was trying to take control, but it didn't work. I went to an Al-Anon meeting, and these three old ladies were talking about alcoholism. I realized they were describing me, and I couldn't face that truth. So I just ran away.

Addiction has many faces, and it's always easier to see it in someone else. Today I am grateful that I finally had the courage to look in the mirror and face my own truth.

—Warrior Priest, U.S. Navy, 1989–1995

MARCH

Talk to Someone

Many of us use alcohol and drugs to cope with our situations. If we decide we can't live that way any longer, though, we need to talk to someone. Because sometimes it can seem like the only other viable option is lead poisoning.

I have a lot of friends who have found that lead in a pistol. So you have to lock those doors.

Call the VA, go to a meeting, call one of your sober buddies—whatever. Many of us feel like we have to deal with these things on our own. But that can be deadly. Just reach out.

When I feel like it is all too much, I will reach out and talk to someone about what I am going through.

—Dan N., U.S. Army, 1971–1977

Pause

I've learned the importance of pausing. I need to pause—especially when I'm unsure about something. I've learned that I'm an extrovert, and my tendency is to just talk, talk, talk. When I'm uncomfortable, I talk.

Back when I was drinking, alcohol filled that gap for me. Now I know to pause and be quiet and just listen. It's so impactful.

I'm at the point in my current job where I'll have all these people—the pharmacist, the doctor, and the research team—coming at me at once. There are days when I'm literally so quiet, because there's not enough time to react to what they're saying to me. They ask me, "Did you hear that?" I'm like, "Oh, yes I heard it. I'm just listening to you, and I'll revisit this in an hour after I've had a chance to look into it."

For me, that is a miracle. Really. Because when you're in the military, everything is quick, snap—right then and there. We have so much coming at us all the time.

For me, meditation has become crucial. I just need to pause and really listen to the universe.

Today I will pause instead of reacting right away.

—Anonymous, U.S. Air Force, 1997–2000

Veterans Helping Veterans in Recovery

Alcohol was my friend and comforter until it wasn't. We all have a bottom. Some are much deeper than others. As a military veteran, I had a hard time asking for help with recovery. We get training in self-reliance and courage in order to get things done.

As a former Marine I was pleasantly surprised to find a former Marine drill instructor as my sponsor and counselor at my first visit to a veterans outreach program after reaching my bottom.

Life has so many better things for us when we ask for help. We are never alone.

Today I will be okay with talking to another veteran, because I know I am not alone.

—Mike D., U.S. Marine Corps, 1970–1974

I Am a Survivor, Not a Victim

I thought I had a simple drug problem until the drugs were no longer a problem. The secret I was keeping was what was really keeping me sick. I never told anyone I was sexually assaulted during my time in the service. I thought that I would take it to my grave, but I knew that I could no longer live silently with this victim identity if I wanted to stay clean. Getting help was the first step. When I learned about military sexual trauma, I found out that I was not alone. When I listened to others, I heard their stories of survival. Now, by sharing my story, I am empowering others to become survivors too.

I don't think about using much anymore. The nightmares are starting to fade. As I put my past to rest, I know the fight is over now. And I am a survivor. If you are reading this, then you are a survivor too.

Today, if I feel like I cannot go on, I will remind myself of everything I have survived to get here. I will no longer be victimized by my past, but I will use my experience to help others and therefore help myself.

—Emil C., U.S. Navy, 1995–1997

A Structured Life

My time in Iraq equipped me with structure. I didn't want to disappoint myself, my leadership, or my friends within my unit.

Upon my return from deployment, I was left on my own to do whatever I felt like doing. I started drinking. How much and how often I drank increased.

When I first chose sobriety, it was a struggle. However, after detox and treatment, I did not let my mind get idle.

I started with small things, like cleaning and reading a book. It was important to be productive while recovering—and it still is. I set and achieve goals that drinking would interrupt.

I am a husband. I am a father. I don't want to let my family unit down. I don't want to let myself down.

When it comes to service and sobriety,
structure is the common denominator.

—Anonymous, U.S. Army, 2005–2009

Finding a Higher Power Is Better Than Playing One

I'm a veteran, and I'm good with talking to veterans. I know some Vietnam guys that I get along with but I still can't get three words out of. I think the older generation is still kind of stuck with the stigma of mental health. "Shell-shocked" and "combat fatigue" are a lot more acceptable. Now, while I'm working with more recent veterans in recovery, it's not a thing where you're looked at in a negative way or like you're weak because you have PTSD or are going to a mental health doctor.

But back when I was in, you did not do that. You didn't want that shit in your file, and you did not go to mental health. Yeah, they debrief you when you get off the plane coming home and ask, like, "Are you suicidal?" And you answer, "I don't know." Then they say, "Okay, you're good to go," and just turn you loose on the world. *Really? I've just been fifteen months, like, playing God. And you're just going to turn me loose on this?*

Screw stigma. Finding a Higher Power is better than playing one.

Today I'll look for the people who have just been turned loose, and I will see how far I've come since I was them.

—Bradley L., U.S. Army, 2005–2010

Different Consequences

I try not to tell people, "If you go into recovery and you're in the military, you're never going to have any consequences."

You're going have plenty of consequences: You're going to be sober. You're going to have a better life. Things are going to improve. You might run into some bumps in the road. But that's not the point.

As I understand it now, the point of getting sober is not so everything in life is perfect. It's so I have a shot at being happy every day and learn to lead life in a way that is more positive for myself.

When I choose recovery, I receive limitless
consequences—positive consequences.

—Matthew S., U.S. Navy, 2006–Currently Serving

Unforeseen Consequences

After my medical release from the Canadian Armed Forces, I was put into a vocational rehabilitation program. Things were good. I went to school on a three-year program for welding engineering, and I flourished. I got a job in the oilfield, bought a house, was in a relationship, and became a father.

When I worked in the oilfield, I was working between two and three weeks on and one week off, sixteen hours a day, seven days a week. This is when I became an isolated and closeted cocaine user. In my mind it was a reward system: *Okay, now I'm going to put my feet up and give it hell.* I was no longer seeking out people to use with; it just became my own thing.

I came home one day, and my house was empty. She left. Took everything. My son was gone. The dogs were gone. There wasn't a spoon left in the drawer.

Still using, I soldiered up, and for a year I managed to refurnish the house and pay the bills. Eventually, I filed a consumer proposal, which is basically bankruptcy. I lost my house, vehicles, everything. It was treacherous.

Today I prefer the consequences of staying sober over the consequences of substance abuse.

—Kory W., Canadian Armed Forces, 2009–2015

Openness

Once I actually answered an online PTSD survey honestly. After I finished it, I got an email saying I needed to come talk to a shrink ASAP. I guess I was in crisis.

The first time I met the shrink, I started sharing what had been inside me for so long. I was on the verge of tears, and I was like, *Where did all this stuff come from?* I really opened up the locker inside. Within five minutes, he was like, "You've got some major issues." He told me I bottle my emotions. That's how I felt—I was numb. I never knew I had PTSD, anxiety, depression, substance use disorder, and the rest.

I've done a lot of therapy since then. I'm grateful that I got the treatment I needed and that I found the VA. Because back then, like so many people, I didn't trust the VA. But it was being surrounded by other veterans that really pulled me through, because they're going through the same things that I went through.

Today I will be open and acknowledge when
I have been numbing my emotions.
I will get help if I need it.

—JR W., U.S. Army, 1987–1995

Showing Myself Kindness

It can be easy to get so wrapped up in trying to fit in that I'm not okay with myself. And so I do a lot of work showing myself kindness and forgiving myself for the ways I think and behave. Being okay with me means not judging every other word I say. It's been pretty difficult since my traumatic brain injury, but it's better now.

I'm a Marine. I was a criminal and a drug dealer, so I can be incredibly inappropriate at times. And a lot of time my jokes aren't appropriate for work. But my supervisor has worked very hard with me on showing myself grace and kindness, and just being good enough. For me this means setting reasonable expectations for myself and letting the process go forward.

Today I will practice not judging myself harshly—
being okay with who I am and grateful
for all I've learned.

—Berlynn F., U.S. Marine Corps, 2009–2011

It Takes What It Takes

In 1986, I was suffering the fallout of multiple affairs that my now-ex-wife was having. I was not handling this situation very well.

Long story short, I accidentally fired a gun into the couch of the living room. Not on purpose. I was drinking at the time. Because everybody cleans their guns while they're drinking scotch on the rocks, right? You know, that's at least what I thought.

But this incident did scare me. It made me think about my drinking, and I decided to go to AA. I liked it! I wasn't drinking, I was feeling good, and I was healthy. For six weeks. Then I figured, *Okay, I've got this! I can do this on my own.*

I didn't get sober then. But it did kick off the beginning of my journey, and I ended up where I am today. Now I sponsor people and I am sober myself.

Today I will recognize that it takes what it takes to get sober. I won't regret the journey it has taken me to get here.

—Ed C., U.S. Army, 1975–1979

You Can Always Find a Listening Ear

I have very close friends in the program. I keep in touch with some who go back to when I was in the Navy. They've seen me grow up in every aspect of my life—especially spiritually. But almost none of them look like me.

Early on, I got accustomed to being the only Black person at a meeting. I've learned a lot from many friends in recovery—especially the ones with a lot of time sober under their belts. But there were certain things I didn't want to talk about with certain people, because I didn't think they'd understand or have an insight, because their personal experience didn't match mine.

We didn't have Zoom meetings back then. Now I'd encourage a woman who feels the way I did to use the wonderful technology we have today to reach out to an online group. Go ahead, chime in and talk to somebody across the world or in another state who looks like you and can relate to your personal experience.

Today I'll use one of the recovery resources available.
I'm grateful that, no matter what, no matter when,
I can always find someone to talk to who
will understand.

—Elora K., U.S. Navy, 1997–2007

A Helping Hand

The first time I got sober was December of 1984. The second time was in November of 1986. I got my orders in July of 1989, and I was scared as hell to move to Tennessee with my two young boys. They were three and five as we were moving across country.

My friend Alonso was like a father to me. He said, "As long as you cover my gas, lodging, and food, I will move you and the boys." He also wouldn't leave until I went to at least one meeting. He wanted me to have my feet somewhat planted firmly on the ground. I did as he suggested.

I'm grateful he was in my corner during this transition in my life.

When transitions in my life arise, major or minor, I will ensure I am spiritually planted with others in sobriety.

—Mary H., U.S. Navy, 1984–2004

Breaking the Rules Can Break You

I was underage when I first went active duty in the Coast Guard, but my wife was a little older, so she could buy our alcohol. Then I got stationed in California but was still able to go to bars and party, because I had a fake ID by then. Where there's a will, there's a way.

A bunch of us had base privileges and got a weekend off, so we rented a hotel room and partied hard. Ultimately, I got caught for underage drinking, because somebody didn't get rid of the beer cans. The Coast Guard gave me a book about what I could and couldn't do—so now I knew how to break all the rules. But breaking the rules eventually broke me, and by the time I was discharged, my drinking was out of control.

It took me years to get the help I needed way back when. But I got sober on December 10, 2010—a date I'll always remember. A date I'll always treasure.

Today I know that while I am powerless over
my addiction, I am responsible for my choices.
And I choose recovery.

—Joe K., U.S. Coast Guard, 1988–1996

This Is All Your Own Doing,
but You Can Make a Change

When I was committed to the VA hospital, I was in such a bad state that I wasn't allowed to leave the hospital at first. Essentially, I was forced to stay until I was cleared to leave. In my head, it was almost like being in jail. Once you're in there, you can't get out until somebody says you can.

That was the big eye opener for me. I had my freedom taken away. But more than that, I realized that this was my own doing! I could stop drinking and using. I could get out of this cycle. It was time to do something about it, or else I would have my freedom taken away again, and I didn't want that to happen. That's definitely what did it for me.

Everyone has their story about what "did it" for them. For me, the time I spent in the VA hospital was a turning point, in terms of coming out of denial.

Today I will be grateful that I was able to let go of denial and address my addiction.

—John K., U.S. Navy, 2005–2009

The Military Begins to Accept Recovery

When I first joined the service, there wasn't really any understanding that some people didn't drink. Others didn't trust me or let me into their inner circles, because I wasn't one of their drinking buddies. Instead, I was given support-type roles. They made me the bartender or the designated driver.

But over time, I did start to feel that attitude change. I joined the service in 1985, and when I applied for Top Secret clearance in 2002, I was actually told that the military wants service members who have identified a problem and are doing something about it.

The winds of change had shifted from my early service days. Recovery is beginning to become more acceptable. At first, we had to hide our recovery. Now, in my experience, it's embraced. These days, many of our chaplains are mental health professionals who are saying things like, "It takes a warrior to admit that you need help." They're changing that whole topic around. Now, instead of pulling yourself up by your bootstraps, they're saying there is strength in admitting that we have moments of weakness.

Today I will think about my sobriety as a path of overcoming instead of a personal weakness.

—J. D., U.S. Army, 1985–1993/1998–2018

Trauma and Addiction Go Hand in Hand

There were times when we'd be loading body bags on a C-17 because we were out of transfer cases. You know, when you see it on TV, you see the transfer cases coming off a plane, and everything always looks so put together. You see the boxes, and it's easy to dissociate from them. But when you have to carry fallen soldiers in body bags, it's something completely different.

This happened on numerous occasions, and for days afterward the pain was so intense that you just want to numb it out—to escape the reality of what you had to deal with. So you drink. Then you drink more. But the pain is still there.

So in addition to being in recovery for alcoholism, I still see a therapist for PTSD.

Today I understand the connection between addiction and trauma. I go forward, one Step at a time, as I continue to heal from the wounds of both.

—Kenneth B., U.S. Air Force, 2001–2007

Freedom in Sobriety

I'm in recovery. And today I'm recovered. Tomorrow I might not be, but today I am recovered. I'm happy—I'm happy in my heart and soul.

I'm capable and reliable now, and people can count on me. They can call me up, and I'll be there. When I was drinking, that was not the case. When I was drinking, I never answered the phone.

But I don't have to live like that anymore. It's such a sense of freedom—knowing that there's nothing pulling me back from living my life. Every day I wake up and I know I don't have to have a drink. I don't have to wonder where my car is. I don't have to wonder who I insulted last night. I am so free. There's so much liberty in that. It's hard to describe, but it's a great deal. That's how I know I'm successful today.

On this day, I will think about the freedom that comes with sobriety.

—Mike D., U.S. Marine Corps, 1970–1974

It Takes One to Know One

When the Navy assigned me to a special State Department unit on a project in Moscow, I was on top of the world and had stayed sober pretty much without AA for seven years. I got on the plane, and when asked what I wanted to drink, I thought, *What the heck,* and said, "Bring me a beer."

I only remember drinking the first beer and didn't come out of my blackout until we landed in Frankfurt. When we got to Moscow, a couple of brass asked if I still drank, and I said, "Oh, yeah, no problem," and took the beer they offered.

Days later, a bunch of us got on a boat for a big, floating drunk down the Moscow River. I invited a gal to the after-party, where I got my beer and tequila, and a Sprite for her. I asked if she drank and swallowed hard when she said, "Nope, I'm a friend of Bill Wilson's . . . I think you are too."

For months afterward, I still drank every day, but I did so with guilt, because somebody had already figured out that I really was an alcoholic.

Today if I meet someone who says they're a friend of Bill's, I will say with enthusiasm, "I am too," grateful for my recovery and the fellowship of AA.

—Mike F., U.S. Navy, 1959–1965/1972–1990

Sexual Violence at West Point

When you're hanging out with a bunch of older people while you're still a freshman at West Point and drinking in the barracks, bad things happen. And for someone like me—when I get drunk, I just want you to like me—suddenly situations get incredibly out of control very fast.

I'm not a small woman. Six foot two, I was 180 pounds and a Division I athlete. I got my ass beat. And then I was raped by two of my classmates. So I had a long weekend at the hospital there at the Academy toward the end of my freshman year. My drinking career was only six months at this point.

And then the Academy said, "Well, if you want to press charges, you realize you're likely going to get kicked out, because you were drinking underage." So I said, "Well, never mind." So I didn't. The next woman they did that to didn't report either.

The woman after that did. She didn't get kicked out. But they did. She had the courage to do that.

Today I will go back to basics and remember the importance of sobriety in my life—despite horrible past experiences.

—Jenna R., U.S. Army, 2005–Currently Serving

Character Defects versus PTSD

Once I started reading about PTSD, I realized all these character defects I had, things people put me down for and things that made it so hard for me to live, were not character defects. They were symptoms of PTSD. That really helped lift my shame.

I mean, I still have trouble with stuff—getting to places on time, employment, terrible nightmares, weight loss or gain, and I'm tired all the time—but at least I know it's not because I'm a bad person. It's because of all the bad stuff that happened to me.

I'm working on that right now.

Today I will continue to seek solutions in healing symptoms of my disease and PTSD.

—Gayle C., U.S. Army National Guard, 1976–1980/1984

Nate

On recruiting duty, I witnessed my best friend in his addiction. He went to the crack house on Friday nights and spent his whole paycheck on getting high. His father was my sponsor. We were looking for solutions, trying to get him sober again. None of them were working.

One night he went home, got in a fight with his wife, said, "I'm going to Louisville to get cigarettes and booze," had a big wreck on his motorcycle, and ended up in the hospital, brain dead. I was present when we made the decision to unplug him. That made a big impact in my life, because I wouldn't be sober without him.

As kids in recovery, we were together every day. When one of us tried to get off-path, we would encourage the other to stay on it. To watch him lose his life to the same thing we recovered from—it tore me up. I wasn't planning on going back out, but his death sure as hell strengthened my reassurance the disease was still out there waiting on me—but for the grace of God, there go I.

His brother and sister are both in recovery and still sober.

Some people will get and stay sober because of the people who died from the disease. Those in recovery are not excluded.

—Joe H., U.S. Navy, 1988–2015

I Drank Every Chance I Got

When I was in medic training, my classmates and I would get together, pool our money, and rent a motel room somewhere. Whoever was legally old enough would buy a bunch of booze, and we would party all weekend.

I remember my first weekend I got absolutely hammered—right out the gate. I was immediately in love with drinking. At that time, I decided that I was going to drink as much as I could.

Any chance I had to go out and drink, I did. The goal was almost always to get drunk. Friends and I wouldn't make plans to go have drinks. It was always, do you want to go get drunk?

I've heard people say, "Drinking wasn't my problem. It was my solution." For me, I always felt socially awkward and like I didn't fit in—like I was a little bit different than everyone else. I don't think that alcohol and other substances took that away or made me feel better per se. But I didn't care as much. You know, it lessened the alienation to a point where I thought I felt comfortable.

Today I will realize that alcohol can be a form of self-medicating, and I will address my discomfort instead of numbing.

—Dennis D., U.S. Army, 1997–2003

I Was a Slow Learner

I was a signalman. I made E-5 pretty fast. I was up for E-6, but before I got promoted, I was at a ship's Christmas party—drunk, of course. The party was pretty dull, when someone said, "Hey, let's start a fight." And, right in front of the captain, the executive officer, and their wives, I sucker punched this young ensign who was a shore patrol officer. As a result, I got a general court martial.

I had a couple of captain's masts and a few DWIs by then. They reduced me to E-1 and sent me to the brig, where I was given a year's confinement and hard labor, but no discharge. Then the judge advocate general reduced it to six months.

I got drunk the first day out of the brig. I hadn't learned a thing. It was 1966, and by that time, I had eight years in the military. I'd like to say I stayed in because I was patriotic, but the truth is it's a great place to party and get drunk.

Today I give thanks that although I was a slower learner when it came to addiction, I was finally able to admit my powerlessness over alcohol.

—Bud N., U.S. Navy, 1957–1983

Addressing PTSD

When I was drinking, I didn't realize that I had PTSD. Mine manifests as a recurring nightmare: in my dream, I'm out on a combat patrol, but the only person on the patrol is me.

So I wake up and feel like there's no one around me; I'm completely isolated, with no one to help. I've been abandoned, even though in reality my wife is next to me and the dog is on my stomach licking my face. The dream conjures up a feeling of aloneness that I just can't shake.

Eventually, I started treating the PTSD after I got sober. I was hospitalized three times in a year. Two for suicidal ideations and one because I wasn't sleeping due to the terrible nightmares.

I have started using meditation to help. First I thought it was total baloney, but one night I was desperate for sleep, so I tried it. Hard to believe, but it worked! Now I use this tool all the time, and it really helps.

Today I will utilize the tools of recovery to
move through areas where I suffer.

—Eric S., U.S. Marine Corps, 2005–2009

Placing My Well-Being First

I was wounded in May 1969—shrapnel in both legs. They sent me to Japan for two months of intensive care and then back to the States. Not long after, I married a beautiful woman who had been writing me letters while I was in Vietnam. That relationship lasted for three and a half years. I felt trapped. She divorced me. Later, in college, I married again. That relationship lasted three years. She left me.

After every failed relationship, my substance abuse got worse and worse. Married a third time. She had a couple of one-year sobriety streaks and a pocket full of thirty-day coins but decided she wanted to continue to drink and use drugs. My sponsor confirmed that I was not only enabling her, but I was jeopardizing my own recovery as well.

We separated.

It was one of the hardest things I've done in my life, but it was something that I had to do to protect my well-being. The separation was important for both of us. Eventually it led to both of us committing to recovery. Next month, we celebrate forty years of marriage.

What I learned is that I need to protect my own well-being even when it means making hard decisions.

I can't want more for people than they want for themselves.

—Doc D., U.S. Army, 1968–1970

Nonverbal Lessons

My last stepdad was a drunk. When my mother passed away, he came to live with me and my family. He kept coming home stumbling. When he fell down drunk in the bathroom, I told my husband to get the drunk out of the house.

About a week later, I'm smashed, and I look in a mirror and have an aha moment. Like, *Son of a bitch, there's still a drunk in the house.* It was a Wednesday night, and my youngest granddaughter came into the living room and said, "What's that funny drinking water?" I said, "What the hell are you talking about?" She grabbed my hand, and took me into the kitchen, and pointed over the stove. I opened up the cupboard and there was a bottle of gin. See, I had decided that if I couldn't handle my wine, I would switch to something I could handle. That didn't work.

But I looked at that bottle and realized I was teaching my kids and grandkids the same exact thing that I had been taught.

Today I no longer have to hide my addiction.
Today my actions reflect my path in recovery.

—Stephanie C., U.S. Navy, 1978–1983

I Woke Up

Before my military career, I had never been arrested. Within six months of returning home from war, I got arrested four times and I couldn't figure out why.

A year later, I received help from the VA for the very first time. I surrendered to the way of recovery through the VA system. Then I went back home.

Welcome back to society. I got a job and an apartment, started working, and had money in the bank. I also got to spend time with my mother that year. Then, on June 12, 2012, she passed away. I didn't know how to deal with that type of grief. Six months after my mother's death, I relapsed and started smoking crack, drinking—you name it. I lost the job, the car, the money, everything. I went back to the VA, and we started the process all over again.

This time I paid attention, listened, and started feeling. I joined Narcotics Anonymous, and I've stayed plugged in ever since. For me, it was almost like waking up to a new life. My clean date is April 17, 2013.

Relapse exposes the lessons learned in our addiction and allows us an opportunity to surrender and wake up to recovery.

—Armando S., U.S. Army, 2006–2009

Sick and Tired

I went through rehab with the VA in New York state. It was the best program. The VA was a godsend for me. Back in those days, probably one or two women had already been through the program there. When I started, I was the only woman, with twenty-six men. They had to block the door when I went to the bathroom. I had a certain time that I had to take a shower.

Coming off the street, I had to surrender. I always think back to that scene. God was already working on me in some kind of way. I wouldn't have been up there otherwise, with all of those men—just straight not talking to nobody; just doing what I do, going here and going to the groups they had, and talking about my problems; just doing everything they told me to do. I also started writing letters asking people to forgive me. I was doing everything.

I knew I had been sick and tired of being sick and tired. I just didn't know it at the time.

Today I choose to surrender and do what needs to be done to sustain my sobriety.

—Karen A., U.S. Air National Guard, 1980–1991

Simplicity at Its Finest

If I wanted to use or drink, I had to play out how I was going to do it. Instead of just accepting where I was at, I used manipulation to get to a place where I thought I needed to be.

I tried to predict outcomes, like how I was going to survive my job. I tried to manipulate my military and civilian bosses, my people, just anybody. That was a lot of work—a lot of continuous work.

Today my manipulations are limited to what socks I want to wear. Really. That's my life. I try to keep it as simple as possible.

When I stay out of the results of any given situation,
I can remain in the present—and keep it simple.

—John F., U.S. Air Force, 1985–1996

Facing the Truth

When I came home from the Navy, I went to some Al-Anon and NA meetings, trying to understand my husband's crack addiction. I'd leave, because it always sounded like they were talking about me. And I wasn't ready to admit I was an alcoholic.

I was making good money at my job, and my husband was spending it on his habit. So I convinced myself the problem was money—that maybe the addiction would go away if I didn't have money. So when my company was laying off people, I asked to be laid off. I could go back to somewhere else and start my life over.

My husband and I separated and I moved with my kids elsewhere. I was happy for a while. Then I had to get a job at a factory to pay bills. It wasn't enough, so I got a second job—first as a receptionist and eventually as a stripper.

And then my alcoholism went into full swing.

I will no longer run from my problems, because alcoholism has taught me the harder you run away, the more likely it is that you will fall.

—Warrior Priest, U.S. Navy, 1989–1995

APRIL

Leaving Service: Debriefing

The military provides debriefings for the transition to civilian life. The material in these classes focuses on securing civilian employment. But this wasn't the kind of help I needed. What I needed help with were the psychosocial, the emotional, and the familial parts. That was the transition I was having difficulty with, and there was nobody to help me.

There was no buddy system where you were connected with someone on the civilian side who helped you adjust or a group of people who would share their experiences with you. You just went to the debriefing classes, checked off the box indicating that you attended the classes, and that was it.

When I got sober in 2007, I couldn't do it alone. I had to get help from others like me—others who had gone through this before—a buddy system. I couldn't just check the "sobriety" box on my life. I had to be open and vulnerable with others.

Today I will listen and learn from other sober people.

—Anonymous, U.S. Air Force, 1997–2000

Spiritual Replenishment

I have a fear of spiritual stagnation. Why? Because the evidence from my time served in the Navy proves it is the first sign of an impending relapse. For me, it equates to the description of a "dry drunk" mentioned in the rooms of AA. Spiritual stagnation makes me coast along in my day without catering to the call of self-care, compassion, and contentment. Simply put, everything sucks.

Sometimes I miss the mark. I don't pray, meditate, or express my gratitude. In turn, the squirrel leaping from one tree to the next appears to be a rat with a feathered tail. The melody of a bird's morning cadence matches that of a mosquito. The sun's beam on a clear day burns my skin with regret, and gratitude is a distant third cousin.

Clearly, sobriety is more than not taking a drink. I can choose to admire the squirrel and the bird, and bask in the sun's rays. Shoot, I can even acknowledge my third cousin as a best friend and greet them with a smile.

When I consciously commit to working a program in recovery, I can embrace life's simplicities.

Spiritual replenishment comes with every pause.
Throughout the day, every day, I will pause
to polish my perception.

—Elora K., U.S. Navy, 1997–2007

Giving and Getting Back

Day to day, I'm able to stay in touch with myself because of the people I work with at the VA. I go and I see what I used to be and where I was . . . and how far I've come and how easy it could be to slip back into that if I get complacent or if I'm not vigilant. And that's a pain in the ass. I really don't like having to be on guard all the time, but it is such a slippery slope.

I'm grateful for the people who I get to hopefully bring back into this world, back to their lives. I get more from them than they ever get from me. Getting to see them every day is a reminder and an inspiration. And sometimes it's heartbreaking, because I've been the guy that just didn't get it. I knew what to do. You couldn't tell me anything. I just wasn't trying to hear it. I wasn't trying to listen. I was so self-centered and selfish that I genuinely believed that I wasn't hurting anybody but myself.

Now I help others while also helping myself.

Vigilance is a pain in the ass, but it keeps me from sliding back down that slippery slope.

—Bradley L., U.S. Army, 2005–2010

Not Your Normal Indoc

Indoc is one of the most important things you can do for an organization when you're about communication. Every week I give a brief on what the media department does, what you can post on social media, the rules and regs, what the ship does, and why your job is important.

One day while waiting my turn after the senior medical officer's brief, there were an E-3, E-4, and E-5 in the training shop with me, and we started shooting the shit. I'm a lieutenant commander, and they weren't used to an officer having a normal conversation with them.

They asked me how I became an officer, and I shared my story of recovery, why I specifically joined the Navy wanting to commission one day, and how it turned my life around.

The E-4 suggested I tell the same story during my brief, because "people actually give a shit about that; they will care about the story you just told us." She was right. It was a bizarre, neat experience. The crowd of sailors went from falling asleep in the back and anticipating chow to questions: "How do I become an officer?" "What was your experience like?" "Are you still sober?" I really enjoyed it.

Sharing our stories of recovery makes a difference within others and ourselves.

—Matthew S., U.S. Navy, 2006–Currently Serving

It Should Have Been Me

I spent years blaming myself for a friend's death. He was standing watch for me when my ship had a main space fire.

It should have been me on that watch, but my friend was helping me out so I could get ready for an inspection. Being an alcoholic in the making, I used that terrible day to dive deeper into drugs and alcohol. It wasn't until I started working a program with a sponsor that I was able to heal. I joined a combat recovery group called Reboot that helped me understand God's hand in all of it.

Recovery for me wasn't just about putting down the substances. It was about clearing the wreckage of the past to genuinely heal. This doesn't mean that I don't think of my shipmate anymore; I think of him daily. But I've learned to forgive myself for something I had no way of controlling. I have learned that if I just remain teachable and continue to seek God's guidance, I can live joyous and free, one day at a time. So I will keep trudging this road of a happy destiny, and surely I will meet some of you on my journey.

Today I will ask for God's will, not mine, to be done.
I will ask for patience in receiving his answer, and I will
forgive myself for things I have no control over.

—Mike P., U.S. Navy, 1988–1992

A Soldier's Calling

When our C-130 touched down on the tarmac in Tallil in Iraq, I took a deep breath. I had arrived. I stepped off the plane and looked around to get my bearings. Off in the distance I saw a church steeple. I thought to myself, *Before I do anything else, I'm just going to go over to that church and say a prayer of gratitude to God for getting me to Iraq safely.*

Once inside the church, my eyes fell on a bulletin board with a flier that read "The Camel Spider Recovery Group of Tallil, Iraq, meets Mondays, Wednesdays, and Sundays." My mind began to reel. Here I was—four thousand miles away from home—and God had seen fit to put me on a combat outpost that had a recovery meeting three times a week. I knew I was going to be okay. I thought about a verse in the Big Book's twelve promises that says, "And God will do for us what we could not do for ourselves."

Some have said to me, "I can't imagine going to war without being able to drink." I tell them, "I can't imagine going to war without the Twelve Steps and a program of recovery."

Today I will incorporate an attitude of gratitude into all of my affairs. I will endeavor to treat others with dignity, kindness, and compassion. I will remember that God is doing for me what I could not do for myself.

—J. D., U.S. Army, 1985–1993/1998–2018

It's Pretty Awesome

While on active duty I received a DUI and took the deferred prosecution. This meant that if I did some things—like go to meetings at least three times a week—it'd be off my record. Recovery really wasn't something I was seeking—until now.

Now I'm actively working a program of recovery, and I love it. Volunteering for recovery programs and meditation are big parts of my life today.

Asking for help is not a weakness. The world of recovery is so liberating. It has given me agency.

Recovery—it's pretty awesome.

I can make my own recovery program—
what works for me and nourishes me.

—Jen O., U.S. Army, 1995–2019

A Better Version of Me

During my addiction to cocaine, I was homeless for almost two years. Literally. Not in a shelter; on the street.

I went to this place run by a nonprofit organization, and they gave us food and clothes every day. The clothes I got for warmth in the winter, I gave away for drugs. They would say, "We just gave you a coat." *Well, I smoked it.*

It was embarrassing, but that was the sad reality of it. That was what I became. That was my smallest me.

Today I choose to reach for the best version of me.

—Kory W., Canadian Armed Forces, 2009–2015

Army Buddies and Sober Buddies: Like Family

Back when I was serving, when you were overseas, your family was not there. Your battle buddies became your family instead. Well, the culture there—the way to bond—was through drinking. If you're not drinking, then you're not really part of a group.

Whenever we weren't in training, we were getting drunk. Then we'd get up the next day and run together, and we'd smell like a brewery. People would have to back away from us because of the pure alcohol sweating out of our bodies.

The thing is, that lifestyle did not serve me when I got out of the Army. My drinking created a downward spiral that led to drugs, which led to being kicked out of my home and living on the streets. The only way I was able to get sober was through the support of other sober veterans like me who knew what I had been through.

Now, with these sober veterans, it's almost like family, because these veterans have been through similar situations as me. I'm four years into my recovery, and I see my sober community as a safe place where I feel the strongest.

Today I will seek healthy community
with other sober veterans.

—JR W., U.S. Army, 1987–1995

From Surviving to Thriving

I like to joke that I spent the first half of my twenties really messing up and the last half cleaning up the messes. Because of all the mistakes I made in the military and after I got discharged, I had to jump through hoop after hoop. I had to write a statement to the Department of Human Services to get cleared to work with people. I had a good job, great credit, and could pay rent several months in advance, but no one would rent to me because of my criminal record.

I was in Veterans Treatment Court, going to college, and working—constantly having to prove myself to a judge, probation officer, or boss. But I hung in there. I learned to advocate for myself.

I guess you could say I went from surviving to thriving. I never thought I'd own a house, earn a degree, or have the job I have. It was a long road, but I made it!

Despite the challenges, I'll strive to do my best in order to move forward.

—Berlynn F., U.S. Marine Corps, 2009–2011

My Life Is Over versus My Life Is Beginning

I was smoking weed, and I was failing the UAs—only I didn't know it. They weren't telling me, so I thought I was doing okay. I thought I was making it.

When they told me that I failed the UAs and was getting discharged, I remember going out to the barracks and lying on the ground staring at the stars thinking, *My life's over. I don't know what I'm gonna do now. This was the game plan: twenty years in and done. I grew up poor in a trailer park with no money and no guidance. Nobody taught me how to do school, so I'm screwed. I'm done.*

The thing was, getting kicked out spearheaded my journey. I went to treatment, then a halfway house. I was sober, I met my wife, went to college, started a career—everything. I didn't know then that I was just at the beginning of the life I dreamed of. But if I hadn't gotten kicked out, who knows where I would have ended up.

Today I will look for blessings in disguise.

—Sean A., U.S. Army, 2007–2011

A Gathering for Two

One day I called my old sponsor. Just before she hung up, she said, "Thank you for brightening my day." I don't know who else called her that day. Maybe it was just me.

Now I have a little reminder in my calendar to call her every ten days. Her husband recently died from lung cancer. She is a brand-new widow and can't go hang out with her peeps, because she's afraid to get COVID. She's around eighty years old, so this is a legitimate fear.

Once every couple of weeks I visit and hang out with her. Sometimes she'll say, "Hey, pick up some El Pollo Loco, and we'll have some chicken in the backyard. You know, if it's cold, we can go inside but during the summer it's nice." I look forward to our get-togethers.

Today my service work will include calling someone to brighten their day.

—Mary H., U.S. Navy, 1984–2004

It's Scary to Get Help

Two co-workers asked me if I thought I had a drinking problem. I said no, because I was really worried about losing my flight status. I was very concerned about my job security in the Navy.

Then my skipper also took me aside and asked me if I wanted to get help. At that point I knew something had to change, so I did a self-referral to the substance abuse rehabilitation program. My skipper had given me a choice, the chance to keep from being pushed aside and thrown away like a broken toy. He gave me the chance to save my family. I was in tears and felt like a huge weight was lifted from my shoulders.

There were a lot of things I was worried about when it came to getting sober, but I ended up getting a lot of support from the military.

Today I will take a look at my fears and think about whether they are preventing me from making a big change in my life.

—Guy C., U.S. Navy, 2005–Currently Serving

Moving beyond Self-Blame

It saddens me that most of my female vet peers have had to deal with military sexual trauma. I'm no exception. I've been sober thirty-one years, and that trauma's something I've just gotten in touch with these past few years.

I joined the Army out of high school, because my parents divorced and I didn't know what I'd do for college. But I knew I had to get out of my hometown. After boot basic, I was in the medical unit at Fort Sam Houston. This is where the first assault happened. I was drinking then, so I didn't even see it as rape. I just turned all the blame on myself. That's when my drinking really took off.

There were a total of three incidents in training, but there was never anybody to talk to about it. And I was afraid of getting kicked out. So I kept on blaming myself. And I didn't get sober until I was off active duty and in the National Guard. It was then when a woman in my unit helped me find AA meetings.

Today I will practice loving myself, because I now know that when I blame myself for trauma that was inflicted upon me, I am blaming the victim.

—Deb L., U.S. Army, 1981–1996

Life after an Other-Than-Honorable Discharge

I had the brilliant idea that if I only used drugs that wouldn't get me in trouble while I was driving; I wouldn't be able to get a DUI. My using escalated after I got an other-than-honorable discharge from the Navy. I was ashamed. You wear the badge of dishonor, no matter how you look at it. I didn't want anyone to know what happened to me in the military. All that hopelessness drove my use, which led me to feel more hopeless, and the cycle continued.

But the truth was I couldn't see that there is a person inside me: the person I was supposed to be before any of this shit ever happened to me. Before I ever had a drug put in my body or any of this trauma.

Now that I'm sober, I stand for things. I have values. Now I know that I'm resilient. I'm here to regain my honor. I've faced my fear of talking about my experiences, because now I know that by sharing I can help people get well too. Opening up has helped me reconcile my past with who I am today.

I remember that I am in the present—not in the past.

—Emil C., U.S. Navy, 1995–1997

The Road to Healing Begins with Self

By the time I turned twenty-one, I had already been drinking for about seven years. I was living on a military base in Cape Cod. One night I went out with some friends and drove back onto base in a blackout state. They towed my car, and I was arrested for operating a vehicle under the influence on a military base. Four hours later, I got my car out of impound and, still drunk, drove it back on base and got another DUI.

Two DUIs in four hours got me into the Coast Guard's risk-reduction program, which meant I was out. They never offered me any treatment—just an honorable discharge.

By that time, I was having a lot of marital problems too. It was ugly—lots of screaming and yelling and unfaithfulness on my wife's part. My wife was from a very dysfunctional family, and I tried to protect her. But it was me who needed the fixing. I just didn't know it at the time. I hadn't yet learned that before you attempt to help others, you first have to heal yourself.

Before reaching out to help someone else,
I'll remember to take my own inventory first
so I can offer my best self to them.

—Joe K., U.S. Coast Guard, 1988–1996

Getting Help While Still in Denial

I did not want to go to the hospital. I didn't want to get help. I had a couple of close friends who were the ones to actually drag me into the car and drive me there. It was a bad scene at the hospital, because they had to call security when we arrived. Four or five guys had to come out and physically drag me inside and then hold me down when I got there.

My journey to sobriety was difficult, and I didn't want to go there at all. I guess you could say I was in denial about how bad things had gotten. But it was good to have those kinds of people in my life—people who knew that something was wrong, that I needed help, and how to get me there. Honestly, I don't know if I would still be here if it weren't for them.

So I am definitely thankful to them for putting me—reluctantly—on this path that I'm so grateful to be following today.

Today I will be grateful for those who have helped me on this sobriety journey.

—John K., U.S. Navy, 2005–2009

My Life Was Spinning out of Control

I knew back when I was deployed that I had a drinking problem, but I didn't realize it was also a mental health issue. I spent a lot of time beating my head against a wall. I went through two divorces, and my life was just spiraling out of control.

There's all this stuff out there—in the movies and on TV—about how people recover from alcohol and other drugs, but I gotta be honest, when I was in it, I didn't know there was any way out. Once I got into addiction, it was full force. For about fifteen years, I didn't have a single day when I didn't drink to excess. I didn't drink socially like most people. They can go to dinner and have a beer. I'm not programmed like that. When I drank, I drank to blackout.

Even if I could have wrapped my head around the idea that people can recover, I didn't know where to start. I didn't get sober until 2017.

Today I give thanks that recovery took me out of the fog of addiction into the light of a new day filled with hope and exciting possibilities.

—Kenneth B., U.S. Air Force, 2001–2007

Pass It On

When I started going to meetings, I realized I couldn't do anything that would fix myself. Thank God for those meetings, because the people in those meetings shared their stories, just like I'm sharing mine. Slowly but surely, I started to come to the point of acceptance.

After hearing all these other stories, I realized that I had a problem, but I didn't know how to fix it. But these people had found a solution. That's what saved my life—those people in those rooms, sharing their stories.

Now that I've found this freedom in sobriety, I have the ability to pass it on, because who knows where I would be if others hadn't passed it on to me! I mean, I'm just so grateful that other people were there for me.

Nowadays I will always be there for anybody who needs me. Because I know where we're all coming from. I will do pretty much anything I can to help them stay on their path. There's a great sense of gratitude for what I've received.

Today I will be open to sharing my story if it will help someone else on their journey.

—Mike D., U.S. Marine Corps, 1970–1974

How Life Changes in Sobriety

When my addiction was at its worst, my biggest hope was that I would die in my sleep. At that time, so much of my life revolved around drugs and alcohol. I would wake up and take a toke off a bong or a sip off a bottle.

Now waking up and having some water or coffee instead of some other mood-altering substance—it just goes to show how getting sober is an entirely different approach to life.

Now I actually have a sense of enjoyment of life again. Maybe it sounds cliché, but there is a sense of serenity that comes with finding recovery, getting some sobriety, and being involved with a program—it's truly remarkable.

Today I will be grateful for the serenity
that comes with recovery.

—Dennis D., U.S. Army, 1997–2003

Alcohol on Deployment

Over time, my drinking kept increasing. I got older, but the drinking never slowed down. It finally got to the point where I was drinking even on deployments.

They say you can't get alcohol on deployments. That's not true, though. There's any number of ways you can get alcohol—for the right price. Oftentimes, the right price was not necessarily monetary in value. But you know, when you want alcohol, that's what you're going to do.

Well, thankfully my life looks very different now. See, one of the things our book says is that, in God's hands, our dark past is the greatest possession we own. Because with it, we can avert death and misery for another alcoholic. And I think that's why I now go down the path of talking to others. If I can share my story and help another alcoholic, then my story has value.

Today I will look for opportunities to share
my story and help other alcoholics.

—Jenna R., U.S. Army, 2005–Currently Serving

A Message of Hope from Me to You

To me it's important to be there to help somebody. Just being able to let them know there is light at the end of the tunnel.

I tell them, find some place to settle down and get involved in recovery—full time instead of hit-and-miss. If you do the stuff that they tell you to do, you'll get there. Don't drink, no matter what. That's like one of those little catchy phrases, but it's true. No matter what happened, don't drink. Don't use. It'll just make it worse. It won't help.

It does get easier. And sometimes it gets harder. You just got to be patient.

Recovery is possible with willingness.

—Gayle C., U.S. Army National Guard,
1976–1980/1984

Sobriety First

In April of 1986, I got sober as a teenager.

Here's a kid who tried to destroy his life, got sober, quit school, and joined the Navy. When I enlisted, everybody said with huge reservation, "Good luck. You're probably not going to make it."

Being the man that taught me everything I know about God, my sponsor told me, "Go live your life; do amazing things. As long as your sobriety's first, then everything will be all right. Go with God, keep your shit together, keep your priorities right, and you'll accomplish great things." And I did.

I served twenty-seven years and was able to stay sober for the duration of my service and accomplish all my goals.

As long as I keep sobriety first in my life,
I can accomplish anything.

—Joe H., U.S. Navy, 1988–2015

Handing It Over to God

When I was active-duty in Moscow, we'd get home and have a few beers and shots every night. On weekends, we'd make the rounds to the other embassies, drinking at each one. I tried to quit drinking a couple of times, or I'd tell myself, *One beer won't hurt me,* but I never had just one of anything alcoholic in my life.

Our main job was to watch the Soviets construct the American embassy and to make sure they weren't planting anything in the walls or ceiling. I'd see them on my computer screen coming back from lunch with bottles of vodka. I could relate to how they'd open a bottle and throw the cap away then drink the whole thing, because that's what I did with whiskey.

In January of '84, I was out drinking on the streets of Moscow and lost the entire weekend in a blackout. I woke up Monday without a clue where I'd been or what I'd done. And it scared me. I slid out of bed, got on my knees, and said, "Dear God help me. I can't do this anymore."

I give thanks that even when I abandoned God in the darkest hours of addiction, he still hung in there and never abandoned me.

—Mike F., U.S. Navy, 1959–1965/1972–1990

Throwing My Life Away

I worked hard at sea in the Navy, but when that ship hit port, some of us guys went out and drank with both hands. It was 1966; they called us steamers back then. I went to Vietnam, and my drinking was out of control. I was getting in trouble but not enough to make me stop.

When I got home, I had shore duty. I tried to be a good dad and husband. I had three kids, and my wife had stuck by me. On weekends, I was a Little League coach, I was a Cub master, I tried to be "that" dad.

But I gave it all up, because drinking was more important. Pretty soon I gave up my whole family, because I chose alcohol instead. I wasn't coming home anymore, and of course my wife filed for divorce. I didn't lose my family—I threw them away.

Hitting rock bottom doesn't mean you have to stay there. You die, or you get help. Today I thank my Higher Power that I finally saw the light and got help.

—Bud N., U.S. Navy, 1957–1983

Leave No One Behind—No Matter the Weight

In boot camp, we had this training where you had somebody on a stretcher and you were told not to leave them behind. Our drill instructors put the biggest guy in the platoon on the stretcher. He was probably about 200 to 210 pounds, whereas the rest of us were all about probably a buck seventy or eighty. We had to carry him for maybe a mile. So there are seven of us total with one in the stretcher. We were rotating in and out who was carrying him with the rest of us resting, and vice versa. That exercise really instilled in me that no matter what the weight is, you have to bring the person with you. You can't leave anyone behind.

When it comes to sobriety, that's what I have found with other sober veterans. When people ask me how I've stayed sober, I make time to answer them and form a connection. I'm not talking about AA though. This is just in my everyday life or in the waiting room at the therapist's office.

There are plenty of opportunities to share hope in our communities. We don't leave each other behind.

Today I will look for ways to share my
hopeful experiences with others.

—Eric S., U.S. Marine Corps, 2005–2009

My Leap

Throughout my drinking life, I taught my children that you drink when you're happy. I also taught them that you drink when you're sad, when you get a job, when you lose your job, when you pay your rent, when you can't pay your rent. I was teaching them the same thing I was taught: This is when you drink. Once you get to a certain age, you're an adult and you drink. That's what I taught my kids.

One day I talked to my husband and told him I needed to go to a program. I needed to go get help. Fortunately, he knew where to take me, because he'd been a cab driver and was taking other people to this place for recovery. He knew where it was and dropped me off.

That was the worst day of my life and the best day of my life.

Taking a leap of faith in recovery is the scariest and most rewarding thing I can do.

—Stephanie C., U.S. Navy, 1978–1983

High Skies

Before the military, I was working for a big company in the hotel industry. I had a very, very good career. One day, I was sent to Chicago on an all-expense-paid trip to train other managers. I was afraid of heights and had never been on an airplane before. When my boss gave me my tickets, I thought it was for Amtrak.

So I went to Chicago. I smoked marijuana before the flights and drank some Heineken during the flights. And I fell in love with heights, with flying.

I fell in love with that adrenaline of fear, which I was not used to. Introduced to yet another thing that I was addicted to—that rush, that feeling of *Man, I might die, and this feels good*—I just became this different person.

That trip ended, and of course things got worse and worse.

Today I can take flight in recovery without a drink or drug—literally and figuratively.

—Armando S., U.S. Army, 2006–2009

God Steps In

I came in with only one bag. The personnel from the VA rehab facility took me shopping. I had holes in my bras. I had no clothes. I had nothing. I later became a secretary in volunteer services. I received awards and was voted in as president by the recovery group. I was like, *What is this going on?* There were just so many miracles happening in my life. And I was like, *This is happening!*

God just stepped in when I walked through that door.

Somebody said that sometimes God reaches out right where you are, pulls you out of that area and pulls you into recovery. You never know where he's pulling you to. You just know when you get there. That's where you belong. That is just what he did to me.

Today let me trust that when I let go and let God,
I am carried to new heights.

—Karen A., U.S. Air National Guard, 1980–1991

Overcoming Fears

I'm working with my Narcotics Anonymous sponsor to go through my Fourth Step again. This time I'm looking at the conditions of my using and addressing them rather than focusing on drug use.

Things are coming out that go all the way back to my childhood. I was molested as a young boy. I drank and drugged to deal with that shit—to survive. I didn't want to share that with anybody, and I held on to it for many years. I became homophobic, I couldn't trust people, and just shut others out. I wouldn't let anybody get close to me.

NA has been a saving grace for me. Through the Twelve Steps, I'm learning how to live my life and deal with emotions and feelings that I ran away from consistently. It works for me.

I also believe that my Higher Power, which I choose to call God, is always with me. I fell. He picked me up and carried me.

While in recovery I can face fears that once plagued me and progress positively toward a new beginning— overcoming, conquering them one by one.

—John F., U.S. Air Force, 1985–1996

MAY

It Doesn't Have to Be That Way

When I first started going to meetings, I was hurting pretty bad. I sat down next to an old-timer. He said to me, "Well." He didn't say the flowery stuff we do nowadays when we talk about getting sober. He didn't give me slogans. He simply said, "Dan, it doesn't have to be that way."

Now, this old man didn't define what "that way" was. Because I knew "that way." I had defined my life "that way" for many years. It wasn't just the drinking. It was the lifestyle that went along with the drinking that destroyed you. But that phrase stuck with me. "It doesn't have to be that way."

There is hope. That is when I decided to go all in.

On this day I recognize I don't have to live "that way" anymore. I can choose a different path for my life.

—Dan N., U.S. Army, 1971–1977

We Are Not the Problem

When people mention your drinking to you in conversation—it's time to get help. When it becomes a running joke that you have a drinking problem—it's time to get help. When people suggest you get help before you get in trouble—it's time to get help. You have a problem. You are not the problem.

Don't wait. Take care of yourself. Find a medical professional. Find a civilian. Find people focused on encouraging you in your recovery.

Support is available to you. When you seek, you will find. When you reach, you will climb. When you try, you will recover in time.

If you're wondering if you need help, no matter the circumstance, the answer is yes.

—Anonymous, U.S. Army, 2005–2009

We Are Not Our Worst Moments

Today I'm able to reach into a place of honesty and really just say, "This is my story, and these are the things that I've done." So many of us are still wrestling with that, trying to find some way to reconcile all of the things that we had to do—or that were put in front of us. And it's difficult.

In the Army I did things that made me feel like I was a monster. When I was using, I acted like one—lying unnecessarily, stealing from people who cared. It's taken a long time to really know that I am not my own worst moments.

I don't want pity. I don't want you to feel sorry for me. I'm a normal person who went through some rough experiences. I'm not a hero and I'm not a charity case. I'm just a person.

It's important to remind myself I'm just a person,
and people can learn and grow.

—Bradley L., U.S. Army, 2005–2010

Stay Connected

I honestly don't have a home group right now. My sponsor is a guy that I had in another state.

If I'm being completely honest, I'm kind of a little bit loosey-goosey right now. Trying to find a home group while you're on sea duty and trying to establish those connections is tough, but I still text with guys that I know in the program. I still stay accountable.

I found a second-class petty officer who's on my ship, and he's been sober for a little while. I've talked to the ship psychologists and the chaplain to figure out who needs help. That helped me, and continues to help me, stay connected and grounded. That's how I've been able to stay sober.

The power of a recovery program extends beyond four walls. Stay connected.

—Matthew S., U.S. Navy, 2006–Currently Serving

The Captain of My Own Ship

Back when I served, the military wasn't helpful when it came to alcohol abuse or addiction. If you confided in a superior officer, or if you got caught acting inappropriately or driving drunk—then you got put into the system. Article 15 or a letter of reprimand or whatever. The military didn't have a path to help us out of addiction.

For me, I realized I needed to be the captain of my own ship. I had to take total responsibility for my own recovery—outside of the military, my family, my business, or anything else. I couldn't blame anyone else for my actions, because the buck stops with me.

But that doesn't mean I'm alone. Recovery is possible, and it has been done before. I mean, I'm coming up on fifteen years sober. But I am only able to get better when I take ownership of my life and take the wheel instead of blaming others.

Today I will be the captain of my own ship
and take responsibility for my actions.

—Terry F., U.S. Army, 1986–1994

A New Path

I served a long time, so I was very familiar with being told what to do.

While serving, I received an alcohol-related incident. The military offered intensive outpatient drug and alcohol programs. It also had inpatient.

Back then, I was really into the Twelve Steps. But there's not just one way to recover. It doesn't have to be that way. We're all unique and different in this community. There are so many different paths. I just love how it's opened up.

For me, meditation and exercise also help. Daily I am empowered to seek out my own path.

I will keep the door of new paths to recovery open.

—Jen O., U.S. Army, 1995–2019

In Transition

Cocaine was my companion. It was more than an acquaintance and closer than a fellow comrade. Cocaine and I had all the time in the world to do what we wanted, whenever we wanted.

The Canadian Army paid out my pension—a lot of money gone in no time, and that was the end of that.

From prestige to the streets: game over. I had nothing to lose.

I went home to my dad's—we barely spoke, and it was not good. But it was a second chance. I dropped the ego and asked for help. There was no way out. Cornered, caught, and had to give in. Miraculously, my family supplied forgiveness, support, and encouragement.

Sobriety calls my name. I have a new hope, new life, and new living.

The physical and spiritual transition
of sobriety is bittersweet.

—Kory W., Canadian Armed Forces, 2009–2015

Asking for Help

Someone asked me, "If you had any advice to yourself from when you were in active addiction, what would you say?" My advice would be to ask for help. Because that's the one thing about the military that hinders us: we don't know how to ask for help.

We're scared of admitting anything. Asking for help was foreign to me. Finally, after my addiction got really bad, I wrote to the VA, asking for help. That was one of the best things that I could have done. I completely surrendered and said, "Yeah, I can't do this on my own."

That step was a big one for me, and it is one of the reasons I got sober. Now I get to help other veterans who come through the VA, once they've asked for help. I got help, and now I get to help others. It's a beautiful thing.

Today I will not be ashamed to ask for help
when I need it.

—JR W., U.S. Army, 1987–1995

I Am Worthy of Being Helped

Everything in the military trickles down. People think they're gonna get out of the military and have a totally different life, but some of the stuff that happened just sticks forever. I was out of the military for almost five years before I even knew what a service officer was or what places I could go to for help.

I had the misconception that what I did in the military didn't matter, which meant that I didn't matter either. I thought I didn't deserve any benefits, which is not the case. Having self-worth is so important, and it is something I'm still working on even after six years in recovery.

Even in recovery, life is gonna happen. But now when I'm having a hard day, I reach out and tell someone about it, because I've learned I do deserve to be helped. I am worthy.

When I am having a tough time, I will seek
and accept the help I need.

—Berlynn F., U.S. Marine Corps, 2009–2011

Drinking in the Army National Guard

My first sergeant during my first drill handed me a bottle. I was eighteen years old. It was tequila, and I put it to my mouth and tipped it back. As I was drinking, this sergeant held his hand under the bottle so I couldn't put it down until I chugged it all. That was my lifestyle prior to enlisting, so my reaction was, *All right, good stuff! Perfect fit. This is where I belong.*

But that was also disappointing, because I enlisted to get away from drinking and away from drugs. One of the reasons I joined up was to clean up my life. Obviously that plan wasn't working out too well, right from the beginning.

When I was kicked out of the Army for drinking and drug use, I was able to use the experience to get sober. I finally did an honest Rule 25 and got myself into treatment.

Today I will be grateful for my story, because it has gotten me to where I am today.

—Sean A., U.S. Army, 2007–2011

The Past Doesn't Define Me

The one thing that the Army did teach me was how to drink. All of my platoon sergeants and platoon commanders were former Vietnam combat veterans, and they taught us youngsters how to drink.

I learned how to become a turtle, and it's just something you really can't explain. You just have to experience it.

I did drink after I served. For many years I struggled with the alcoholic habits I formed in the Army. But nowadays, things are different. I'm sober. I live in a rural area where the cows outnumber the people. I go to meetings and talk on the phone to people seeking recovery. I go fishing with my granddaughter.

I had to learn these new habits by sticking with other sober people. Nowadays I recognize: You're gonna make mistakes; we all make mistakes. And then you say, *Well, we're not gonna do that again.* That's where the Serenity Prayer comes in.

Today I will recognize that the past doesn't define me, and that it's okay to make mistakes.

—Ed C., U.S. Army, 1975–1979

Claim Your Freedom

In the military, someone else is always calling the shots. How you dress, where you go, who you are with, what you do, and even what secrets you keep are all determined by people and things outside of your control.

But right now, no matter where you're at in life, you have freedom over your recovery. You are the only person who can make the decision to heal. The fact that you are reading these words right now shows that you are aware of this. At the very least, in this area of your life, you have all the freedom you need.

Today I encourage you to claim that freedom. Figure out what claiming your freedom looks like for you, then commit to that life, because you are worthy of it.

I have the freedom to recover however works best for me.
Today I remember that I am worthy of that freedom,
and I claim it as my own.

—Anonymous, U.S. Army, 2009–2016

We Understand This

So far, you're ahead of the rest of them. You understand life and death. You get "A day at a time." You know how to work as a team, from varied backgrounds, but now that doesn't matter.

You know that people who stay connected stay alive. You understand "team." You understand that people are much braver when they are together than when they're alone. You understand survival training.

People aren't shooting at you now, but it's just as deadly. The very fact that you're here, in front of me, shows me that you have strength. Resiliency.

I will remember: "Yea, though I walk through the valley of the shadow of death, I will fear no evil, for I am the baddest motherfucker in the goddamn valley."

—Don E., U.S. Army, 1967–1970

Making Amends Is an Exercise in Humility

After I got discharged from the military, they hired me under contract as a secretary. Nothing against secretaries, but it took a lot of courage for me to go from being an air traffic controller second class, training over twenty people at my last duty station, to being hired to track their records and all that stuff.

I was making progress in the program when my sponsor told me, "Okay, it's time to make amends to people." I was still learning to knock down my pride, so I was like, *Oh my gosh, I see these people all the time. I've cussed some of them out in the past.* But it's about accountability, right?

So I was pulling people aside at work, one by one, to offer amends, telling them I'm not the same person I used to be and asking them what I could do to better our relationship. Some said, "It's okay. We're cool." But others told me, "You can do these things," and I had to swallow my pride and do it.

Today I'll practice what AA teaches about humility:
"Humility isn't thinking less of yourself but
thinking of yourself less."

—Elora K., U.S. Navy, 1997–2007

Forgiving Yourself

I was drinking heavily, and one day I was supposed to pick my son up from school. I didn't make it to the school to get him. The thing was, my wife was out of state, so she couldn't get him. In the end, one of my neighbors had to step in to pick him up and keep him for the night while my wife tried to find a flight back home.

That whole time, my son thought I was dead. That made an impact. If there's any story he tells about my drinking, that's the day that he reflects back on.

I would do anything to take that day back. But I have to accept that it happened. That's part of living with your consequences. I had to forgive myself for that.

On this day, I will work toward accepting my past and forgiving myself.

—Guy C., U.S. Navy, 2005–Currently Serving

Embracing the Family We Create

I think having an alcoholic dad and seeing him go downhill and how it screwed up our family was a catalyst for me getting sober. I had sort of a head start on recovery, because I'd gone to Alateen and Al-Anon as a kid. I was in the service when I finally had to face the fact that I was an alcoholic myself.

I was at the point where either I had to get sober or I would kill myself. So I decided to try the sobriety option. I was in California, and my whole family was in Alabama, so I was there pretty much alone. This was actually a blessing, because they weren't there to enable me. I was on my own to go to meetings, and friends in recovery became my family.

Today I know that family isn't just about bloodlines.
Today I give thanks for the family I have created
in recovery.

—Deb L., U.S. Army, 1981–1996

A License to Get High

After I got out of the military, I started using cocaine and heroin. Soon after, I broke my back in a motorcycle wreck. I got prescription pain medication. This gave me a license to get high, all while I was still trying to squash my trauma and escape my pain.

I would try to escape by working a hundred hours a week. Using and working, working and using—trying to escape myself. Everywhere I went my trauma was there. I couldn't get away from it. The need to escape led to new levels of what seemed acceptable. When you're trying to find ways to get drugs, you're living in this continuous escape cycle. I was isolated, and I was in a place of despair and darkness.

But now that I'm in recovery, I find that support and connection is the opposite of addiction. I'm connected now, and no one lets me go for long without getting in touch. And I do the same. I'm always trying to connect with people. I am a hundred percent plugged in, and I love it.

Instead of getting high, I connect with others in recovery. I don't need to escape anymore.

—Emil C., U.S. Navy, 1995–1997

Seeing the Light after Blacking Out

I experienced both physical and sexual abuse as a kid and was already drinking to blackout by the time I signed up for the Coast Guard at seventeen. My drinking didn't let up in the military; there was more trauma there as well. I got some DUIs on the base that ended my military career.

After my discharge, I got a job as a flight attendant. It was a wonderful way to travel and drink with my coworkers. We partied hard, and I'd usually drink until I was able to pass out. At one point, I had been drinking with the crew and went outside to smoke and blacked out. A good Samaritan found me, and I woke up at a hospital. A doctor said I was lucky to be alive, because my blood alcohol was over .49 percent when I came in.

About twelve years into that job, I finally decided it was time to clean up my act. When I went to treatment in Minnesota, my life changed. I've been sober now for twelve years. I say I got my degree at alcohol college. It's definitely given me the tools I need to stay sober. I've just gotta remember to open the toolbox.

Trauma accumulates, but substance use is not the answer. Recovery can't erase the trauma, but it can help us carry it differently.

—Joe K., U.S. Coast Guard, 1988–1996

Drug Life Felt Normal

For me, drugs had become such a part of my life that I didn't feel normal when I was sober. My first relapse happened because I thought, *Okay, it's time to get back to life as it normally was.* For me, that meant living in an altered state.

I slipped and made the call. I got the drugs, and that turned into a two-week-long binge. When I was in a relapse, I remember feeling that getting high was being "normal" again. But after about two weeks, I started to get the feeling that I was losing my grip again. So I had to stop and realize that being high cannot be my normal life anymore.

Actually, that relapse was an educational experience, because I had tried to go back to what I knew, what felt familiar, and where I felt safe. And it just turned out to be the same thing that I was trying to stay away from to begin with. If I go back into that same rut, I'm going to get the same result.

Today I will take lessons from my bad experiences to help me craft the life I want today.

—John K., U.S. Navy, 2005–2009

When We Step into the Rooms, We Take Off Our Rank

Sometimes I'll be in a meeting with other veterans and they'll find out that I'm a retired major. And they start calling me sir. Then I say "It's John," and then they'll respond "Yes, sir." It's a habit that is hard to break. It's like if someone named Mr. Reed was your fifth-grade teacher: if you ever run into them, they'll always be Mr. Reed to you, and not Jerry or something.

I sometimes run into a senior officer that I served with, and I refer to him as sir automatically. We do that as a sign of respect. But when we get into the rooms of AA, we take off the rank, and we're all just alcoholics. You will see sometimes that they'll still look at you in a leadership role. But ultimately, we're all just humans who have an addiction problem.

On this day, I will remember that everyone is equal in recovery.

—J. D., U.S. Army, 1985–1993/1998–2018

Accepting Help

When I was in the military in the early 2000s, alcoholism and drug addiction were the kiss of death. If you liked what you were doing and wanted to keep on doing it, you certainly didn't say you had a problem, because that was pretty much it. If you were using illegal drugs, you were probably going to jail if they caught you. If you were an alcoholic, you were probably on your way out.

At one point in time, there was this really great sergeant who could really see inside people, and he saw there was a problem. He referred me to what at that time was called a BAP (behavioral analysis program), which was basically an IOP (intensive outpatient program) for active duty. The only reason I did it was fear of getting kicked out, because I didn't think I had a problem.

It's not that BAP didn't try—it's that I wasn't ready to recognize I had a problem. I didn't graduate from it, because another deployment came up. The idea was, *Well, he's going overseas, so he won't be able to drink over there. That will fix his alcoholism.* Nothing could be further from the truth.

Today I'll remind myself that help is always there when I need it, but I have to accept it for it to do any good.

—Kenneth B., U.S. Air Force, 2001–2007

Getting Out of God's Way

I fell off the wagon when I was stationed in Moscow after nine years of white-knuckle sobriety. I drank every day there. After spending an entire weekend in a blackout, I was finally scared enough to go to my boss for help.

In 1984, there was a policy established for the military that if you had a problem with alcohol or other drugs, and came forward before you got into serious trouble, there would be no disciplinary action. So they put me on a plane back to D.C.

I got there about one in the afternoon and made it to an AA meeting at four that same day, where I raised my hand as a newcomer and said, "My name's Mike, and I'm an alcoholic, and I need to know how to get sober." A guy next to me said, "Why don't you try prayer?" I said, "Like that's gonna do me any good." He tapped me on the shoulder and said, "Who the hell do you think has been keeping you sober since you got back?"

Today I'll remember that I not only have to
get out of my own way, I need to get out
of God's way too.

—Mike F., U.S. Navy, 1959–1965/1972–1990

Dream Big

I think when alcoholics get sober, we sell ourselves short. We don't think we can accomplish the big goals. We dream small. And I tell people all the time not to dream small. Why do we have to live like we're second-rate citizens? It's almost like we have this preconceived notion that, as alcoholics, we can't accomplish certain things because we have emotionally beaten ourselves or been beat down. It's such a terrible disease on so many levels.

When I got sober as a kid in '86, I was able to figure out I didn't have to live like that. I just kept doing what I was supposed to do, every day: dreamed big and tried to make a difference.

I've achieved so much more in my career and my sobriety than I ever thought I could. It still amazes me today, but I owe it all to the fundamental things I learned when I got sober. In my alcoholism, I couldn't even have dreamed this big, but I got sober, and my level of gratitude is off the charts.

Why can't you dream big?

When we work a recovery program, we embrace
and embark on our biggest dreams.

—Joe H., U.S. Navy, 1988–2015

Alcohol Stopped Working for Me

When my rock bottom happened, everything fell apart. I wasn't working, and my mental health was out of control. I assaulted my wife and went to jail. Then I became homeless for a while, but I used that homelessness to get loaded all the time.

Eventually I realized that the drugs and alcohol weren't working anymore; they weren't making me feel better at all. There was no element of fun or enjoyment to drinking—it was just making me feel worse. I was getting suicidal, which scared me enough to talk to my therapist. I ended up doing forty-five days inpatient, and that was my first introduction to AA.

The way things changed for me after that is remarkable. The ninth promise of AA says we will have a new attitude and outlook on life. For me, that has come true. There are still difficult days, but my life is so much better than it was.

Today I will think about my rock bottom and the way my life is different now that I am sober.

—Dennis D., U.S. Army, 1997–2003

Facing the Truth

After I lost my wife and kids because of my drinking, I married a bartender I was playing house with. I thought it would be a marriage made in heaven, because she drank just like me, but then even she said I drank too much.

I was doing shore duty at that time and had made chief petty officer. I promised my captain and I promised my wife I wouldn't drink. But I never really quit. By that time, I was 356 pounds with a fifty-four-inch waist and had to have my uniforms tailor-made so I'd look good. So, after twenty-two years in the Navy, they finally sat me down and said, "Chief, you have a problem," and they sent me to a weight control program at Long Beach Naval Hospital.

Once I got there, this counselor looked at my file and saw all the captain's masts, all the DUIs, and the time I spent in the brig. It was like watching slides of all the degrading things I had done. He asked if I had an alcohol problem. I wanted to answer no, when I heard a voice from somewhere saying, "This is your last shot." And, for the first time in my life, I believed it and admitted that I was an alcoholic.

I went to the hospital as an overeater, and caught alcoholism while I was there.

Today I give thanks for the still, small voice that finally led me out the darkness of addiction.

—Bud N., U.S. Navy, 1957–1983

Addressing PTSD

When I was drinking, I didn't realize that I had PTSD—mine manifests as a recurring nightmare: In my dream, I'm out on a combat patrol, but the only person on the patrol is me. So I wake up and feel like there's no one around me; I'm completely isolated, with no one to help. I've been abandoned, even though in reality, my wife is next to me and the dog is on my stomach licking my face. The dream conjures up a feeling of aloneness that I just can't shake.

Eventually, I started treating the PTSD after I got sober. I was hospitalized three times in a year. Two for suicidal ideations and one because I wasn't sleeping due to the terrible nightmares.

I have started using meditation to help. First I thought it was total baloney, but one night I was desperate for sleep, so I tried it. Hard to believe, but it worked! Now I use this tool all the time, and it really helps.

*Today I will utilize the tools of recovery
to move through areas where I suffer.*

—Eric S., U.S. Marine Corps, 2005–2009

Share the Joy and Sorrow

My problems seem significant until I compare them with other people's. When I have a problem, one of the first things I do is call my sponsor or someone else in the program. The Big Book tells us that there's nothing more effective than working with other people to keep us from wanting to take a drink or use drugs. When talking about our problems, the moment the words hit the air something magical or mystical happens. And it changes everything.

At my father's funeral, I quoted a Swedish proverb that says, "Shared joy is double joy; Shared sorrow is half a sorrow." When we share our problems, it allows other people to help bear those things.

We don't have to bear the burdens by ourselves.
When we share our problems, it allows other
people to help bear those things.

—Doc D., U.S. Army, 1968–1970

Spiritual Warfare

In my addiction, I did all kinds of stuff with all kinds of people. Then, of course, I got into trouble and got caught. It was ugly. I got locked up, arrested, the whole nine yards.

Then my time came up to end my military contract. Did I want to stay or go? I decided to throw in the towel. I wanted to come home. When I came home, I thought it was going to be okay. I thought that I had left war behind—not only the war that I had just come from, but the war that I had been fighting my entire life.

I didn't know that I brought the war back with me— in my head, heart, spirit, and soul.

*Recovery heals me and brings peace
in times of internal warfare.*

—Armando S., U.S. Army, 2006–2009

A Good Foundation

After I left the VA treatment program, I was in a town in New York, close to New York City. The cost of living was a little bit higher than I was used to. I couldn't really afford an apartment for a single person.

At six months sober, I had to go back to court. They said I did so good with the program that they wanted to help me get my kids back. I declined. I said, "I'm not ready." I told the judge, "I'm afraid. I don't have a foundation of recovery yet. And I feel that if I don't have a foundation I might use again. Six months is not enough time for me to get my children back. I don't have a place to live, and I really need a good foundation. I haven't started doing any work on myself foundation-wise or Step-wise, because I haven't started doing my Step work yet. I think I really need more like a year—almost two years of clean time. I don't want to use again."

They understood, and they gave me more time to work on myself before I got my children back.

A good foundation in my recovery serves as a good foundation in all areas of my life.

—Karen A., U.S. Air National Guard, 1980–1991

My Fellowship

There was a voice in my head—I call it my addictive voice. It called out like, *John, let's try this. Just do this.*

Early in my addiction, I avoided situations that triggered me and brought out this voice. I don't necessarily avoid these situations today. The difference is I have people around me holding me accountable. I've learned how to have fun. I hang out with people who are recovering.

For instance, if we go watch a football game, we walk into the event strong in numbers. Even though people are drinking right next to us, we take soda, water, iced tea, and other non-alcoholic beverages. We have as much fun as the people drinking alcohol. To each its own.

I thought sobriety was going to be boring, but you know what? My life is so much more exciting! I get to have relationships back in my life. I get to go places. I get to do things. Instead of isolating, I get to be part of a community. My fellowship is my fellowship. And you know what? My addictive voice is fading day by day.

Today I get to share an exciting life of sobriety with people just like me—fellowship is fascinating.

—John F., U.S. Air Force, 1985–1996

Money Wasn't the Problem

The adjustment to civilian life wasn't an easy one. My husband and I split because of his addiction and other problems, and I was living with my three kids in Texas. My way of avoiding my own addiction was to just not have money. If I didn't have money, I couldn't pay for it.

I eventually met up with someone at the bar who wanted to take care of me, and he moved in with me and my kids. He was an alcoholic, and the cycle repeated. Even though I drank a lot myself, I could stop when I wanted. But I always seemed to end up with people in my life who couldn't.

I was in Al-Anon for years even though I still drank. Eventually I had to admit I was also an alcoholic.

Today I am grateful that I finally realized money was not the root of my problems. Alcohol was.

—Warrior Priest, U.S. Navy, 1989–1995

JUNE

Starting to Change

Sometimes it just takes one person to initiate a change. After I rejoined civilian life, a neighbor in my community noticed that I was having difficulty. She saw me sitting on the stone wall in front of my house, having been up all night drinking. I looked like a mess. I didn't even know this woman; she would just see me outside.

One day, she approached me and said, "You don't have to live like this." I didn't know what she was talking about. But she convinced me to go to a meeting.

I went to a meeting and thought, "I'm not anything like these people. I'm not coming back." Then a week later, I would drink and feel terrible. So I would go to a meeting again. I would go to a meeting and I would say, "I can't identify" and "I don't have a problem." Then I would drink and wonder, *Maybe I do have a problem.*

It took me a few years to get sober. But the slow change came about, and here I am.

Today I will be open to the small steps
needed to make big changes.

—Anonymous, U.S. Air Force, 1997–2000

Be Gentle with Yourself

Use the resources that are out there to assist you. We get medical help for physical ailments but frequently ignore the psychological ailments; I know I did for too long. Seek out the most qualified therapists, the finest treatments and therapies.

For a long time, I did not want to let go of the nightmares I lived through. They were like good friends that you could rely upon to feel something. As I progressed into healing, the memories remained but failed to maintain their negative influence. They're still there, just in a different spot.

I grew up in the seventies. A poem by Max Ehrmann was quite popular then. It is called "Desiderata." I want to share my favorite lessons from it with you: to be gentle to ourselves as children of the universe and, whether or not we see it, the universe is "unfolding as it should" and we have every right to be here just like the trees and stars and everything around us.

I bid you peace.

Trust that you are a child of the universe.
You have a right to be here.

—Ed C., U.S. Army, 1975–1979

Find Your People

While I was serving in a transition unit, I was surrounded by people actively trying to heal. When I called for help, they answered. When I talked about my challenges, they believed me. When I faced difficulties, they strengthened me.

The more I met with them, the more relief I felt to be part of a group actively seeking and pursuing recovery.

It was a different kind of camaraderie. With them, I was more than a person who had a drinking problem. With them, I experienced renewed confidence and trust in my peers and leadership each day.

Serving in a unit like this I felt welcomed, included, and comforted.

Surround yourself with the right people.

—Anonymous, U.S. Army, 2005–2009

Speaking the Darkness into Light

I'll always have this darkness in me that I just carry. It's just my burden, and I can't put it on anybody else. I can't blame it on anyone else. I signed up, and I'm responsible.

We are notoriously the silent type, tight-lipped. We don't talk about it. "We don't feel," like we say in the military. I used to say, "I had a feeling once." I remember that one time, and that was it. I shut that down. We're just expected to be this way, which is why it's hard to break through.

But what I've decided is that if my story can help one person—I don't ever have to meet them, I don't ever have to talk to them—if they just hear something I said or something that I wrote, I can believe that everything that I went through has value. If I could just change one person, even a small bit, it was worth it.

Today I will not stay silent and tight-lipped.
I will share my story with myself to spread
my own light within me.

—Bradley L., U.S. Army, 2005–2010

Doing Service in the Service

At twenty years old, I completed boot camp and transferred to Navy A School for initial job training. The Liberty organization encouraged sailors to have a good time with their friends in the Positive Student Peer Program. Conceptually, the incentive to the command was less alcohol-related incidents. If we didn't drink during our time in training, we'd receive an "attaboy" from the commanding officer.

When the advisor of the program transferred, I was asked to run the Liberty activities. The problem was I didn't have any money. I was broke from all my stupid behavior before I joined the Navy. Even though I had a suspended license, I decided to grab a fifteen-passenger van every weekend and help the community outreach organizers on base. On Saturdays, we'd feed the homeless at a church, work for the American Legion cutting grass or doing shrubs, or visit with kids to talk about service. We did all sorts of things and I loved it.

One: the "attaboys" were great. Two: it kept me out of trouble. Three: I was doing something for somebody else—giving time, energy, and effort away to another human being. I know it helped me thrive.

When I focus on serving others, I receive the greatest benefit—a purpose-filled life.

—Matthew S., U.S. Navy, 2006–Currently Serving

Will I Be Judged If I Don't Drink?

Before I quit, I wasted a lot of time worrying about what other people would think if I started to turn down drinks. I didn't know how to explain why I wasn't having a beer at a barbecue. How was I going to survive a nice dinner out without a bottle of wine?

But now, on the other side of it, I can tell you: no one gives a hoot! If you're trying to improve your life and you're trying to be a better military member or husband or father or businessman, then what other people think if you turn down a drink should be the least of your worries.

When I quit drinking, I saw an incredible, immediate increase in the quality of my relationships and my effectiveness at work. Sure, in the past, I enjoyed drinking. But by quitting alcohol, my sobriety has had a substantial positive impact on every aspect of my life.

If I worried about judgmental people, I would have missed out on this opportunity to become the best version of who I can be.

Today I will leave the judgment of others to the
side and focus on my own recovery.

—Terry F., U.S. Army, 1986–1994

To Blame or Not to Blame?

The answer is easy: to FORGIVE. The task to forgive wasn't simple and required courage, but it is part of the path to recovery. On the same day that my wife told me, "I'm not excited for you to come home from deployment," my peers said junior sailors were talking about me drinking all the time. And it was starting to affect work. I was filled with regret, which was on my mind long before the intervention because of my many bad choices.

I experienced the ensuing shame and guilt, including the loss of my "fit-for-duty" status. Being told that I was medically "down" was a humbling experience. I realized that only my actions over time would help others accept me. Finally, as I worked the Steps, my cravings subsided and the feeling of suicide was no longer an option, because I learned how to forgive myself. Today I live an honest life without regrets and am medically cleared and fully reinstated, selected into the ranks of senior leadership, and given positions of trust. Sobriety through AA works! Hold your head high, serve your country with pride. It's your DUTY!

Have I forgiven myself, or am I just suppressing my guilt?

—Guy C., U.S. Navy, 2005–Currently Serving

For Better or Worse

As my addiction progressed, instead of snorting lines I was smoking crack—heavy.

When I moved back home to my dad's, I ran into a girl I grew up with, and we were selling it to support our habit. It got way out of hand—just being lazy and not wanting to be a productive adult because we wanted to get high and sell it all day. I made dumb choices and was losing control.

As a Canadian veteran, I begged and pleaded with Veterans Affairs for help, programs, grants, or bursaries to go to school or job fairs. Anything. Their response was always "Call back" or "Email us and go on your account." Little did they know I didn't have a cell phone, because I gave it away for drugs. I didn't have a laptop for email, nor did I have a vehicle anymore.

I felt there was no one I could talk to. I couldn't get out. I was committed to my addiction in tons of bad ways. It was a deep, deep hole I couldn't get out of if I wanted to—or so I thought. But I was wrong.

Today I am committed to the present.
Today I am committed to my recovery.

—Kory W., Canadian Armed Forces, 2009–2015

Leaving Service and Processing Trauma

When we leave service, so many of us get out thinking that we can just take off the uniform, put it on a hanger, and then start living in the real world. But it's not that easy. Because a lot of bad things happen during our tours of duty. I went through a few things that desensitized me, and I wasn't the same person when I left.

I've seen body bags zipped up. We tend to take the bad things that happen during our tours and we lock them up in a hurt locker in the back of our head. Then we never ask for help, because asking for help while you're in the military is considered a red flag. Well, that's part of the reason we lose so many veterans to suicide every day.

We need to work on making it acceptable for soldiers and veterans to ask for help. One thing we can do, as veterans, is ask for help. Reach out to the VA or local sobriety meetings or someone in your social circle who has worked on their own addiction. Look into therapy. Just don't suffer alone.

Today I will reach out if I need help.

—JR W., U.S. Army, 1987–1995

Shame and Fitting In

The first nine years of my life, I grew up in a trailer park. People called me trailer trash, dirty Mexican. When we moved away, I still felt that stigma attached to me.

There was one time I was getting beat up on the bus, and this big guy came and started beating up the guy who was hurting me, and he said, "Hey, come sit with me." So after that, I rolled with their crew, even though they were bigger than me and seemed like tough guys.

I have learned that one of my MOs is to seek out people who are in a higher position of power and have them shelter me under their wing. Even though I would seek people out, that shame prevented me from really connecting with anyone. I didn't know how to get past it.

Eventually, when I got into recovery, I found out that I could go ask people for help, and they will help me! I wish more people realized that. Because I didn't realize I could actually ask for help until I got sober.

*Today I will reach out for help and address
my feelings of shame from my past.*

—Sean A., U.S. Army, 2007–2011

Your Choices Are Powerful

Everything that happens in the military—both good and bad—is like dominoes in a line. Every slipup, every achievement, and every assignment can have long-term consequences for our careers and our families. Your choices in recovery are just as powerful, if not more so.

When you need to feel grounded in your decisions, ask yourself: Who am I spending my time with? Am I working the Steps? Am I taking care of my health? Am I being honest about where I'm at?

In the moment, these decisions might seem small, like they won't make a big difference. But your success is built on "small" choices. Just like you've been told to take sobriety one day at a time, break it down even more: make one choice at a time.

Today may I have an open and clear mind to make the right decisions for me. When I'm restless, anxious, or uncomfortable, may I find the strength to focus on the next right choice, one decision at a time.

—Anonymous, U.S. Army, 2009–2016

Rediscovering God

I grew up in the church, but I didn't have much of a relationship with God. After I got discharged and was a few years sober, a preacher who is like a grandfather to me shared his story. "I used to drink just like you," he told me. "But for the grace of God."

It blew me away. I had known him since I was three and had no idea. I took it as a sign that I needed to return to church. He encouraged me to do that. I was broke and homeless, living in my truck. I weighed about a hundred pounds at the time. I had even shaved off all my hair, because I couldn't afford Black hair products. I was residing in Corpus Christi; he got in touch with another preacher there and suggested I attend the church's Bible study and "see what happens."

So I walked in and—along with my blood relatives and AA—they soon became my third family.

Today I'll trust that when I'm lost and in despair,
there will be someone or something to steer me
in the right direction. I only have to look for the
signs that show me which path to follow.

—Elora K., U.S. Navy, 1997–2007

Fun Times for All

In my early sobriety, I made sure my kids had several outlets, from therapy to Alateen. My sons would join me at conventions, and they loved them. There was an ice cream social on Friday nights.

When I was working at the Alano Club, they visited and played pool. My youngest son learned how to play from a guy who was an old, retired alcoholic on dialysis. As an adult, my son later moved to Las Vegas and became known on the intermediate pool circuit. He still talks about the man that taught him how to play pool.

They had a lot of fun.

As I grow in sobriety, my recovery extends to my family in fun ways.

—Mary H., U.S. Navy, 1984–2004

Alcohol Does Not Discriminate

There are alcoholics of every stripe. Everybody has the picture in their head that a drunk is somebody who's underneath the bridge with a brown bag. Sure, some of us are like that. But there are all kinds of alcoholics out here. I am a naval flight officer, and it happened to me.

Alcohol doesn't care about your sex, your race, or your job. It doesn't matter who you are. Alcoholism impacts people from all walks of life. The stereotype needs to change, because it can prevent people from getting help.

I never could have just one drink and be done, not even when I was a teenager. Recognizing these things sooner in our lives can save us a lot of suffering. If we change our understanding of what an alcoholic is, some of us may be able to quit earlier and have a much higher floor than others did. We can recognize the signs and get help.

Today I will be grateful that I was able to recognize the signs of my alcoholism and get help.

—Guy C., U.S. Navy, 2005–Currently Serving

Making Peace with the Past

After I moved from California to North Carolina, I found a nonprofit that works with at-risk youth. They also worked with veterans, but I didn't go there as a veteran. I went as a volunteer to help everybody else, because I didn't think I needed help myself. I was in AA but hadn't yet come to grips with what I had experienced in the military.

Then one time they had us all go around and say who we were. A lot of people said they were veterans, so I told them I was too. They asked why I wasn't taking advantage of the programs they had for veterans, so I started going to them. When I did an immersive retreat, I ran into somebody I served with in Germany.

I started taking back a piece of myself then—the part I had thrown out when I had left the military, angry and disillusioned. I stopped working with kids and started doing more with veterans. And I did more for myself as a veteran.

Today I am grateful that recovery has helped me reclaim those parts of my past I treasure and given me strength to deal with the pain and trauma I experienced.

—Deb L., U.S. Army, 1981–1996

Use and Lose

Twenty-plus years of using. It didn't happen overnight, but eventually I lost everything. I would use, and I would lose. It was an endless cycle, and I went all the way to the bottom. I lost my job, my marriage, the house. I lost my father. I lost my brother and sister to overdose and my mom because she was using. You would think I reached rock bottom, but it just kept going to the next level of a new low. You always have a new low.

Addiction is a progressive disease. It's chronic, progressive, and fatal. It always gets worse, and there's no magical cure.

I got sober partly because my probation officer did an intervention with me. I had knocked out in the lobby of the probation office. She saw it as a cry for help, and I finally saw the opportunity to try something different. I decided to seize the moment and take whatever I could get from what was offered to me.

Hitting rock bottom helped me try something different for the first time.

—Emil C., U.S. Navy, 1995–1997

The Vicious Cycle of Addiction

Long after I got discharged, I was still drinking and blacking out. I tried to stop drinking on my own, but that only lasted a couple of months. Once I dipped my toe back into the water, it was off to the races again.

Alcohol was my first love, but I also did cocaine, because the more cocaine you do, the more you can drink. So I always found a way back to my first love. Then I'd wake up and feel like shit, so I'd do more cocaine.

I destroyed a lot of relationships because of my addiction. "Normal" drinkers didn't stand a chance in my life. I'd choose people who would enable my use and help me cover up so I could hold down my job.

That cycle continued until I ended up in the hospital after another blackout. I knew then I needed help or I'd eventually end up dead. That's when I checked myself into a treatment facility as an inpatient. That decision saved my life.

When it comes to addiction and recovery, there are
helpers and there are enablers and saboteurs.
Today I surround myself with those who support
my recovery and applaud my growth.

—Joe K., U.S. Coast Guard, 1988–1996

Writing to See the Bigger Picture

I actually write quite a bit and I think maybe there are some veterans like me who feel the same. I personally like to write poetry a lot.

I don't know if others feel the same, but for me, writing is a great outlet, and it helps me get my thoughts out there. Writing helps me think about my experiences and process what I've been through. Sometimes there are things I am not even aware of, but putting my thoughts on paper helps me see the bigger picture. Plus it's a creative outlet, and it helps me when I've been feeling stuck.

Today I will grab a pen or a keyboard and put my thoughts down when I need to.

—John K., U.S. Navy, 2005–2009

When the Solution Becomes the Problem

I was diagnosed with severe combat-related PTSD and alcoholism, but I still wanted to be the one driving the train, so to speak. So I refused to go to inpatient treatment at first. But my train totally went off the rails, and I knew there was absolutely no way I could do this on my own.

I ended up at a VA dual-diagnosis facility for six months. I had been using alcohol to numb the pain and reduce the anxiety from PTSD. I thought alcohol was the solution. It worked for a while—until the solution became the problem, and I couldn't leave the house unless I was intoxicated. I finally just threw up my arms and started listening to people. I couldn't deny it anymore.

After I got into rehab, my head started to clear. And when I stood up for the first time at a Twelve Step meeting and said, "My name is Ken, and I'm an alcoholic," I felt a tremendous weight being lifted from my shoulders. It was the first time in years I was actually telling myself the truth.

Today I will remember that when the solution becomes the problem, it's time to get help.

—Kenneth B., U.S. Air Force, 2001–2007

Play the Tape All the Way Through

In AA, I was taught to "play the tape all the way through." What does that mean? Well, say you go to a wedding or a party, and all of a sudden you look at that drink and you get this euphoric recall. You remember how nice the first drink was and how it made all your muscles relax.

AA has taught us to play the tape all the way through, because if you don't, you're gonna go take that first drink, and you're going to get relaxed. And if you don't play that tape and see how it ends—with me in jail and no driver's license, wanting to lie down in the street—then you may well end up taking that first drink. So anytime I see a drink, I play the tape all the way and see where I'd be if I were to drink it.

Today I will think about the consequences of my actions.

—Mike D., U.S. Marine Corps, 1970–1974

Taking a Moral Inventory

After treatment, I was stationed in California. I went to AA, but was still pigheaded about asking for help. I could do the first three Steps. I could admit I was powerless over alcohol. I believed God could restore my sanity. I could turn my life over to him. Then I got stuck. If I didn't do Step Four pretty soon, I knew I'd get drunk.

I went to a meeting and said I needed to know how to work the Fourth Step, but I didn't get much help. But afterward, a guy took me aside and said, "I want you to go back to your quarters and read the Third Step like it's laid out in the Big Book. If you can then do the Third Step prayer, you'll be ready to start Step Four.

I did what he said. Then I got on my knees and did the Third Step prayer just as sincerely and honestly as I possibly could. I could feel something come over me, and I started writing. I wrote and wrote. Not the best moral inventory I've done, but it was the start.

Today I'll take my moral inventory as a way to hold myself accountable and chart my growth.

—Mike F., U.S. Navy, 1959–1965/1972–1990

Consequences of Alcohol in the Army

One day, I decided to down some beers on my way to learning how to slide down ropes out of helicopters. So I had a freak accident on an obstacle at Air Assault School where I should not have gotten hurt. Suddenly I found myself falling nine feet flat on my back. I broke multiple vertebrae; I tore a bunch of muscles and practically severed my sciatic. I didn't move for forty-five minutes, because I couldn't. I did some pretty bad damage to my back.

But here's the best part. All of a sudden now I am getting meds that are legal. Docs can prescribe opioids—as much as I want—because I am in so much pain. Now I'm taking the meds with the alcohol. Lord knows what the hell is going on in my head.

I will say, the accident advanced my addiction quickly enough that when I went to the military hospital for help, the counselor looked me dead in the eye and said: "Major, you not only have severe alcohol use disorder, we need to send you to the ER now. You're being recommended for at least a week of detox and then inpatient treatment." That turned into three and a half months of treatment, which, in turn, saved my life.

Today I will remember all it took to bring me to sobriety.

—Jenna R., U.S. Army, 2005–Currently Serving

Thank God for Old-Timers

I never changed my home group, because I was so connected to it. To this day, it is the oldest group where I'm from. All those old-timers in that group meant a whole lot to my recovery, because they accepted me as a sixteen-year-old kid and encouraged me.

When I say "old-timers," I literally mean people with like twenty, twenty-five, thirty years of sobriety. Some people don't have a community with old-timers when they get sober. When they first talk, you're like, *These people are crazy,* because you don't relate to anything. Nothing makes sense that comes out of their mouths. You just look at them and think, *They've been sober a long time, so some of it must be true.* When the miracle starts to happen in your life, you realize how important those people were later—if you stick around long enough.

Thank God for old-timers, because when I was able to start putting one foot in front of the other and things started to get clear, I could really see what they meant all along.

I am grateful for the wisdom, patience, and selfless service of the old-timers. Their life lessons in recovery pave the path of hope.

—Joe H., U.S. Navy, 1988–2015

Checking My Ego at the Door

The name tag they gave me at the naval hospital where I went for treatment read "Bud Light." We all wore our uniforms during the day and civilian clothes at night. After I checked in, I walked into a room where this E-5 said, "Oh, good. New man in the room cleans the head." And I said, "I'm gonna find out who's in charge of this place. Chief petty officers don't clean heads."

I went out into the hall, and there's this guy vacuuming. His name tag read "Happy Hank." He said, "Hi, Bud, can I help you with something?" When I saw that Happy Hank was a rear admiral, I said, "Yeah, I've gotta find some stuff to clean the head."

So that was my introduction to treatment. And humility.

Today I'll check my ego at the door and practice humility. As they say in AA: "Humility isn't thinking less of yourself; it's thinking of yourself less."

—Bud N., U.S. Navy, 1957–1983

Getting Sober without AA

For me personally, I haven't sought out Alcoholics Anonymous for my recovery. I went to a veteran center and participated in groups there. I also got therapy. After my second hospitalization, I got started on meditation, and that's what has helped me the most.

I also use prayer, which has been helpful to me when I've needed it. There have been times I've struggled, and then I've prayed. For me, reaching out to my Higher Power did minimize the struggle. It helped relieve some of that stress or anxiety that makes challenges even harder to overcome.

I get a lot of help and support from my wife as well, and the veterans in my community. These connections with other people help sustain me and keep me on the right path.

On this day, I will seek out whatever tools
I need to help me stay sober.

—Eric S., U.S. Marine Corps, 2005–2009

My Sense of Peace

I was going to meetings probably for a couple of weeks before I could say the word *alcoholic* in the same sentence with my name. I saw an old guy there who had a peaceful look in his eyes. He had what I wanted—that sense of peace. I didn't have that.

Along with being an alcoholic, I was disabled. With PTSD, survivor's guilt, wounds, and diabetes from Agent Orange, you know, in all I rated about 90 percent disabled. Though the real math of the percentages for each of those items didn't really add up to 90 percent, under the VA they did. I hate VA math. It doesn't work for me. And this contributed to my lack of peace.

The thing is that, even with my disability, I'm able to give back what I found in the program, and that's critical to me. That peace of mind is worth so much. There's not a day goes by that I don't see some of those images that I saw in Vietnam. But they don't manage my life anymore. And that's critical to that peace. That peace of mind.

I'm able to give back what I found in the program,
and that's critical to me. That peace of mind
is worth so much.

—Doc D., U.S. Army, 1968–1970

Drinking to Suppress

I'm the only one in my family who graduated, but Navy boot camp showed me something different. It opened a door to the opportunity or the ability to be more. I took pride in that. I was never in trouble in boot camp. My motto was "Keep my mouth shut and just go forward." And I did—I learned that at home.

After boot camp, I got orders to Hawaii. I didn't want to go, because the love of my life was in Tennessee. When I got those orders, he said cynically, "You know your mom's going to be happy." The only thing that would have made my mom happy was for me to not be with him, because he was Black. He was doing everything right in our relationship, and leaving him just tore me apart. I drank and drank and drank.

Today I am grateful I no longer have to drown my sorrows in a bottle or a drug to numb the pain.

—Stephanie C., U.S. Navy, 1978–1983

The Best Gift

I gave my sons two dads. It's the one thing I believe is the best gift a dad could ever give his children. They have their stepdad, and they have me.

When it comes to how I grew up and how they're growing up—how they can receive love and give love—it's a better life than the one that I lived.

I wouldn't have been able to do this with my old mentality and my old ways of thinking and living. If it was all going to end today, I think I would be okay with it because they smile. They have what I didn't have: love, life, family, friends, and security—everything that everyone, all human beings, should have.

So let's just say that I'm grateful.

Today I will dedicate time to contributing to a better life for myself. In turn, I can help create a better life with others.

—Armando S., U.S. Army, 2006–2009

Set the Example

When I had about eleven months clean, I needed to move to another town in New York for work. This town was also closer to my sons. I started working for the One Stop program there and started going to college. That's when I began the transition to getting my children back.

I continued to see them on a monthly basis. They started staying with me every two weeks. This included unsupervised visits, because the court system knew I was clean. Everything was open and aboveboard.

One day the judge asked to have my sons join me in the court and had them sit on each side of me. The judge started the hearing by pointing to me and saying, "This is a person who has done everything that is supposed to be done when it comes to what we ask a person to do to get their kids back. This young lady got clean. She's got a job. She's got a place. She's in college. When we asked to give her kids back, she said she wasn't ready." He meant them to understand I was doing the right thing by taking the extra time to strengthen my recovery.

Today I will set the example of doing the next right thing in my daily walk—not only for myself but also for others.

—Karen A., U.S. Air National Guard, 1980–1991

Do the Right Thing (Again)

It all starts with doing the right thing. I just tried. I practiced until it became good behavior. It became a routine every day. For me, that's where it all started.

Then I built a conscience. Something as little as not throwing a gum wrapper on the ground. I get to a trash can.

That's what I had to learn. That's how I had to learn. Developing new behavior patterns. This is recovery.

Today I will practice the next right thing. Tomorrow
I will practice the next right thing. I will continue
this path, no matter how slight it may seem
to the outside world.

—John F., U.S. Air Force, 1985–1996

JULY

Getting Our Self-Respect Back

I met a man in jail. He was a Vietnam helicopter pilot with a silver star. I said, "What are you doing in here?" He was a senior NCO with a big chest full of medals. But there he was, incarcerated.

It's hard to transition from service to civilian life. When you get out, you lose your unit and your rank. You've gotta find gainful employment, reenter your family life, and all the rest. Well. We weren't given the tools to do that. Instead, some of us use the same destructive tools we used in the service: booze and drugs. We go down a dark road and lose even more self-respect.

When I meet these men in jail, I ask them their rank. Then I use it to address them. This gives them back that self-respect, because without that, you aren't going to get far. I give them someone to talk to, who can guide them. I share how I got sober and how it can work for them too.

They begin to gain hope about their circumstances. They see their self-respect come back.

Today I will remember the importance of self-respect and how recovery can bring it back.

—Dan N., U.S. Army, 1971–1977

My New Job

After rehab, I attended an outpatient treatment program for more drug and alcohol counseling.

When I returned to my unit I didn't have a place. I was the guy in the shadows. Because I didn't actively participate with the unit, I received the third degree from my peers. Not many of them understood that I was healing from an internal, undetectable injury.

When they deployed, I was transferred to a Warrior Transition Unit that was dedicated to recovery.

It served people healing physically, mentally, and emotionally. This unit became my new place. My mission was my recovery.

No matter the time or place, recovery is my mission.
Recovery is my duty.

—Anonymous, U.S. Army, 2005–2009

Owning My Life

In the military, our lives are not our own. The same can be said for my drug addiction. I lost every sense of who I was, what I stood for, and what I believed in. Instead, who I was—what I stood for and what I believed in—was my next fix. I didn't think beyond that moment.

Through both of these phases of my life, I felt the need to reclaim myself. I needed to feel that I mattered and that I was not just a face in the crowd or a statistic. I am a man with a compassionate heart, an old soul, an affinity for music with powerful lyrics, and a deep and undying love for my families.

So today I have reclaimed my life and built upon it. I help other veterans by being the person that I needed that I could not seem to find. And I found that person, because I reclaimed the good man inside of me.

*Today I will be mindful of what makes me a special
and important person that others can count on.
And a person who can count on himself.*

—Bradley L., U.S. Army, 2005–2010

A Leap of Faith

I was concerned about the impact my past was going to have on my application for Officer Candidate School. I thought you had to be this perfect person to be a naval officer. So I talked to my AA sponsor about it. Me: Hey, Bill, I want to apply, and I think I found a path to get there. There's a thing in the application about moral turpitude and whether or not you have good morals.

One week later—Me: Bill, I don't think I can do it. I think somebody is going to shut it down. Two weeks later—Me: Bill, there's no way it's going to work. Bill: Hey, Matthew. Do you want to be a naval officer? Me: Yes, Bill. I want to be a naval officer. Bill: Then fill out the fucking application. I'm tired of listening to your shit. Just fill out the damn application. Me: Okay. Roger that.

It turned out my division officer was in recovery and saw what I was trying to do. He knew where my heart was, could see me going in that direction, and facilitated the process. I received my commission.

Sometimes we need an extra push from others
to take a leap of faith toward our dreams.
Take a chance with change.

—Matthew S., U.S. Navy, 2006–Currently Serving

Big Dog in the Military

I was an Airborne Ranger. I did a lot of cool stuff. The military taught us to lean forward in the foxhole—to be a proactive leader, to be macho, to become what you wear on your shoulder and your chest. Your credentials and your rank determine who you are.

The military benefits from this mentality. But there is a human cost. When you get out of the military, you have to redefine who you are. If you build a business, start a family, or whatever you're doing, your rank doesn't matter anymore. But the big-dog mentality hangs on.

Some people have an easier time processing their return to civilian life. But for me, that big-dog mentality was a net negative and contributed to my drinking. I had to redefine myself in civilian life, which is an entirely different way of being.

Recovery gives you the opportunity to define yourself and choose how you want your life to go—outside of your past, your credentials, or the big-dog mentality. You get to decide what path you want in life.

On this day, I will choose my own path,
and I will let go of the big-dog mentality.

—Terry F., U.S. Army, 1986–1994

A Design for Living

Basic training taught me what it was like to not only be part of a team but part of something bigger than myself. In AIT, I discovered alcohol. I got completely hammered and was immediately in love. I looked forward to any chance to drink from then on. My bouts brought me into many close scrapes, but managing to avoid serious trouble was all the excuse I needed to keep on.

My drinking sped along the turbulent end of my first marriage, and a few years later defined much of my second. Eventually serious trouble did come, and I lost everything. Desperate and on the verge of suicide, I went through treatment and joined AA.

I got a sponsor and eight months of sobriety, then threw it away thinking I could control my craving for weed. Numerous slips proved me wrong. I realized there would never be enough to feel good—and became truly willing to go to any lengths for sobriety.

AA's Twelve Steps helped me better understand myself, my disease, and others. I will never be cured, but today I have "a design for living" that works in rough going.

Do I have a design for living that works
in rough going today?

—Dennis D., U.S. Army, 1997–2003

My Calling

I want to practice what I preach. I want to be a success story.

At my worst, I shit the bed completely. Now I'm at the top again. I want, by the grace of God, to get a job where I can talk to people about recovery as work. That will help my sobriety 100 percent. I know it will. It'll help me, but in return I'll be helping people as well. Whether it's one or one million, I don't care.

I have to be a little bit selfish, because this is for me. I need to be sober and be the best me. But while I'm doing that, if other people jump on that bandwagon, that's cool. This is my calling.

Because recovery is possible, my river of hope is broad. My wings of wonder are limitless.

—Kory W., Canadian Armed Forces, 2009–2015

Battle with Addiction

Sometimes I like to think about myself being in a battle with my addiction. My addiction is trying to make moves on me, and I'm countering. I use the skills that I learned in the military to combat my addiction. Like an enemy soldier, my addiction is not going to go away just because I put the bottle and drugs away. It's always going to be in the back of my mind.

But today I'm able to utilize what I've learned in the military to plan for that. Everything I do in recovery helps me build another brick in the wall to where I'm building up a defense against my addiction.

Today I will suit up and show up in life to stay one step ahead of my addiction.

—JR W., U.S. Army, 1987–1995

Second Chances

After getting discharged, my life kept going downhill. I was so broken. And I was a drug addict. I was like a caged animal backed into a corner. I felt like I had to fight— that's what you do when you're backed into a corner.

I had a criminal record and was probably looking at about five years in prison. But they sent me to Veterans Treatment Court instead. If I were them, I would have thrown the book at me. But they took a chance. They believed in me.

I was in that program for a long time. You have to have six consecutive months of verified sobriety, and if you miss taking a drug test, you start over. I lived in a sober house and went to NA meetings every day. I made friends, and they brought me to more meetings. I built a support network who taught me that people are worthy. And the more clean time I had, the better I felt about myself.

Meetings. Meetings. Meetings. Support. Support. Support. Say it with me. Then do it.

—Berlynn F., U.S. Marine Corps, 2009–2011

I Believed I Could Do It; I Just Needed the Tools

After boot camp, I quit all the "hard" drugs. Somehow the military taught me that I can do anything that I believe I can do. It's just a matter of believing I can do it. I learned that given the tools, given the resources, and given the direction, I can execute on things. It's just finding the tools, resources, and direction to help me make big changes in my life.

I learned through the military that if someone has done it before, then I can do it again. If they did it, I can do it too—I just need to learn how to put those pieces together.

I found those tools through treatment and then in Alcoholics Anonymous. But people get tools from other places. One of my sponsees goes through this church-based recovery system, and that works for him. I'm open to these new things now. I want to learn about it and see all the people getting sober too, because there isn't just one way; there's not only one set of tools available to get sober.

Today I will seek out the tools that can help me sustain my recovery.

—Sean A., U.S. Army, 2007–2011

Recovery Takes Work

When I wanted to stop drinking, I asked, "What do I have to do to get sober?" They said, "All you have to do is one thing." I said, "Really? What's that?" They said, "Change everything about yourself."

It was well worth it. It was well worth the change. I do three or four meetings per week now. My day starts with prayer with my second cup of coffee. I jokingly say that God has asked me not to speak to him before my second cup of coffee. So I honor that request. I read the Third Step Prayer, the Eleventh Step Prayer, and I read the thought of the day from the Hazelden *Twenty-Four Hours a Day* book.

Recovery takes effort, and it takes work. But if you were in the Army or the Marines or the Air Force—any branch of service—you're strong and you did it. You survived it. You got your discharge, so go forth and make a difference. If you make a difference for yourself, you will make a difference for other people. And that's all I got to say.

Today I will remember that nothing changes if nothing changes, and I will put work into my recovery.

—Ed C., U.S. Army, 1975–1979

Connect with the Folks Who Understand

While serving, we've got a lot of eyes on us and every move we make. In the moment, it's not always great, but it does mean someone is looking out for us.

In civilian life, no one cares if your shoes are tied or if your shirt is ironed. No one is really watching you or looking out for you. It's up to you to reach out and make those connections.

Recovery is not a journey you are meant to take alone. Connect with veterans and active-duty service members in your community. We understand each other without having to explain ourselves. We can still look out for each other and hold each other accountable when needed. Find folks who understand. Find the ones who will fight alongside you.

I ask my Higher Power to help me to remember that while at times I may feel lonely, I am not alone. Guide me to find others who will understand my trials and triumphs.

—Anonymous, U.S. Army, 2009–2016

Sing Your Own Song

For me, music is a spiritual experience. I grew up in a household with music around me all the time. I listen to everything from opera to Jimi Hendrix. There's always a song that can express how I feel when I don't have the words.

There was a time in my drinking—especially when I was stationed in Sicily—when I would put on gospel music in particular. But I would have a bottle of Hennessy with me. It was the only way I could cry. I'd call out to God through music but felt like I couldn't communicate to him without a drink. Hence the gospel music.

In sobriety, music allows me to cry and talk to God without alcohol. I began thinking of love songs as God singing his love to me, or me singing my love to God. I still love gospel songs. I learned early on in church how these songs let you identify with the struggle and let you know, although you may be hurting now, there's light at the end of the tunnel. There's joy in the morning.

Today, through music, I'll open myself to God's love and the love around me, letting "this little light of mine" shine brightly.

—Elora K., U.S. Navy, 1997–2007

Alcohol Is Everywhere

Alcohol is everywhere—especially in the military. You can't go to hail or farewell without it being at a brewery. You can't go to a party without there being tons of alcohol. You can't go to a dining-out and have nonalcoholic grog for everybody; most people would probably roll over dead if that were to happen.

When I was drinking, I always had the perception that everybody was drinking as hard as I was. They really weren't. And then when I stopped drinking, I was worried about how others would treat me when they saw I wasn't drinking with them at these events. It turns out that people just don't care how much you are or are not drinking. I was always worried about being the guy that didn't have a drink in his hand. Today that's not an issue.

On this day, I will consider that perhaps the stigma of being a nondrinker is not as big a deal as I once thought it was.

—Guy C., U.S. Navy, 2005–Currently Serving

The Miracle of Recovery

Until I started getting grounded doing trauma work with horses, I didn't realize how severe my PTSD was from the trauma I experienced all those years ago in basic training. Or how disconnected from people I had become. I had gotten sober, gone to meetings, and gone to a spiritual center, but I didn't start dealing with my trauma until I incorporated horses in my recovery. That's when things got real. That's when I realized that all this stuff I thought was me was actually trauma.

Now the me that I was before the military is finally coming back around, and I don't have the shame and guilt I had. I'm reconnecting with parts of myself that had just shut down because of trauma. A therapist at the VA has helped me tremendously; one in Asheville probably saved my life.

I was able to have a great visit with my mom over Thanksgiving. I was estranged from her in high school and lived with another family during my senior year. We were still estranged when I joined the military. This time I didn't feel anxious or irritated. I felt like I was in my body. It was just beautiful. That's the miracle of recovery.

I go forward with body, mind, and spirit intact,
thankful that recovery has offered me a way
to reconnect with myself and others.

—Deb L., U.S. Army, 1981–1996

That'll Never Be Me

There are always new levels of what becomes acceptable to you when you're trying to find ways to get the next fix and to get more. It's an endless escape cycle.

I always thought I would never use the needle. Then one day, here I am using needles. I didn't consciously make the choice to become homeless and addicted— it just happened. When it does, you know nothing. *That'll never be me.*

I didn't know why or how, just one day what was never imaginable became acceptable to me. But recovery was always in the back of my mind.

I am making a conscious choice to choose recovery and accept that recovery saved my life.

—Emil C., U.S. Navy, 1995–1997

New Life, New Friends

When I finally entered treatment after drinking pretty much nonstop for over sixteen years—including my time in the Coast Guard and at my job after discharge—my life changed. So did my relationships. I met a guy in treatment who I immediately bonded with, and we're still really close friends. We've gone to every annual reunion, and he and his partner are coming to my place for Thanksgiving.

This recovery thing isn't all peaches and cream, but it has become a lifestyle. I still have to work on controlling stuff; if I don't get my way, I can still be an asshole. This can be rough, but I wouldn't even be here to tell my story if I were still drinking and using other drugs.

I've been able to rebuild my relationships and establish trust with those who are most important to me. It's amazing.

> *Today I give thanks for my recovery and the*
> *amazing friends I've made because of it.*

—Joe K., U.S. Coast Guard, 1988–1996

I Can Control How I React

I was in the Navy for four years. I was an engineer and so I worked on the ship's generators, air conditioning, and refrigeration.

I was expecting to be stationed in Texas, but once I got there, I was immediately deployed to Bahrain. I had just gotten married and I expected to spend some time with my new wife. It turned out that we spent our first year of marriage apart from each other.

Being stationed in Bahrain was definitely not a fun time. There wasn't a whole lot to do. Basically, we lived on the ship next to the pier, and we would go out to sea and come back—that's it. Besides that, we would pretty much just drink, because we missed home and didn't speak the language.

I didn't like that I wasn't in control of my life when I was in the military. Now that I'm sober, I realize that I do have some control over my life when I choose not to ingest drugs and alcohol. I may not be in control of the external factors, but I can control how I react to them.

Today I will focus on what I can control in sobriety.

—John K., U.S. Navy, 2005–2009

Freedom and Sobriety

Thomas Jefferson put it this way: "The price of freedom is eternal vigilance." That adage inspires me. But I've changed it up a bit to fit with life in recovery. The way I frame it is, "With sobriety comes freedom, and with freedom comes responsibility."

This means that you need to follow whatever your program is. You need to be honest and fess up to any mistakes you've made. And you need to live your life in a responsible way. If you do those things, you will be happy, joyous, and free. That's what recovery costs, and it's well worth the price.

Today I will be responsible in order to maintain the freedom I have in sobriety.

—J. D., U.S. Army, 1985–1993/1998–2018

Acting As If

"My name is Ken, and I'm an alcoholic." That one simple phrase opened up a lot of doors of recovery for me. When I told that truth, the first three Steps—admitting my life was unmanageable; understanding there was a power greater than myself; and turning my will over to that power—came soon after. It was liberating.

When I walked into the rooms of Alcoholics Anonymous and heard other people telling their stories, I felt like it was the first place, in a long time, where I finally belonged. They were vets, just like me. And if they could do it, so could I.

One of the first things they told me when I got sober and started going to meetings was to find somebody who has what you want and stick with them. One guy gave me a lot of hope. He had been sober three weeks. For me back then, being sober three weeks would be like winning an Oscar. And he was happy! That's what I ultimately wanted—happiness. I thought, *Man, if this guy who had also been to Iraq and Afghanistan can do it, maybe there's hope for me.*

I don't always have to have the answer right away; acting as if the possibility for happiness exists helps me move in a positive direction toward achieving it.

—Kenneth B., U.S. Air Force, 2001–2007

Bulletproof

Back then, I had just gotten out of the Marine Corps and I didn't think anything could stop me. I was indestructible. Bulletproof. If I could talk to myself back then, I would say, "Be real and look at yourself. What are your goals and where is your life taking you?"

Because at that time, I was just going down the road, you know, blindly. I didn't have an outside view on myself and my choices. I was just plowing ahead—drinking and doing my will and running my own life. I actually thought I was doing great!

Honestly, that bulletproof mentality has faded over the years as a result of the consequences my drinking has brought me. I know now that, yes, in fact, alcohol can stop me. I am actually not as bulletproof as I thought I was.

Today I will recognize the gift of vulnerability that brings awareness and self-reflection.

—Mike D., U.S. Marine Corps, 1970–1974

When the Student Is Ready, the Teacher Will Appear

I went to AA every day on the base, had done Steps One through Four, but still didn't have a sponsor. There was this guy with about twenty years of sobriety who seemed to know what he was doing, and he agreed to hear my Fifth Step. We went to the beach, and I talked for over an hour. Then he said, "How about the take-it-to-the-grave stuff? Nothing works unless we get all of it."

I told him my deepest, darkest secrets and felt a load lifted. Then he told me to read and think about what the Big Book said about Steps Six and Seven. That's when my recovery journey really began.

As the saying goes, "When the student is ready, the teacher will appear." Today I give thanks for all the teachers I have had throughout my journey of recovery.

—Mike F., U.S. Navy, 1959–1965/1972–1990

I Was There

I've been sober more than I've been drunk in my life. As a parent to three amazing daughters, I've been able to be a steady father figure. It means a lot to me, because I didn't grow up with a good father. To be able to be there for my kids—good, bad, or indifferent. To be consistent is awesome.

I'm able to talk to them about mental health. I understand sickness and disease. I've been able to not only show through my actions but also talk them through their rough patches—some pretty serious; in different stages of their lives, they were each suicidal. Because I'm in recovery, I was able to say, "I can relate. I understand. Have you thought about this? Have you thought about that? This is what I do." I wouldn't have been able to do that without recovery.

It's been very rewarding for most of my life—and I can say I was there.

Today I will be present for my loved ones—
sober in mind and spirit.

—Joe H., U.S. Navy, 1988–2015

Denial, Drinking, and Depression

I have had depression and anxiety for a long time, but I didn't have a name for these mental health issues. I just knew I was unhappy. On top of that, for many years I was in denial about my drinking. I would tell myself things like *I'm just a heavy drinker. I just like getting drunk, and that's normal.* When you're in the military, it does seem normal, because almost everyone is doing the same thing.

I have been sober for a few years now, and I still struggle with depression and anxiety. But now, instead of getting drunk when I feel down, I've gotten pretty good at getting up and going outside. I take a walk, I write my feelings on paper, or I call somebody on the phone to talk about it. Plus I have my two cats, who are loving and cuddly, and spending time with them gets me out of my head and focused on something else.

On this day, I will recognize that there are healthy ways to address depression and anxiety instead of using substances.

—Dennis D., U.S. Army, 1997–2003

Mental Strength Gained from Time in Service

When I was detoxing, I was having the shakes and cold sweats. I wanted to drink a beer or have a shot or something. I told myself I couldn't just keep saying *no, no, no* in my head. So I poured a shot.

I set it down, and I stared at it sitting on my counter. I stared and stared for five whole minutes. I was deciding what to do with it. Finally, I dumped it down the drain.

I believe the military gave me the mental strength to push through in that moment. Because I knew that if I took that shot, the whole thing would start over again, and I didn't want that. So I had to dump that shot. I had to own that this was my problem and I had to do something to fix it.

Pouring that shot out felt freeing, because instead of something having power over me, I had power over myself.

On this day, I will rejoice in the freedom that sobriety has given me from alcohol and other substances.

—Eric S., U.S. Marine Corps, 2005–2009

The Development of Spirituality

I grew up in a very strict religious family. The God of my youth was a God with a lot of rules. And if you did certain things, you were gonna burn in hell forever. And that didn't sound like a lot of fun, and, you know, when I gave that up and came into the program of recovery, I got to choose a loving God. And you know, as the years go by, it's less important for me, in my limited cognitive ability as a human, to understand someone that might have created the world and the universe and everything else. So I try to keep it more simple than that.

If nothing else, when I had that sense of desperation, when I need spiritual help, the program of recovery is spiritual. We have a spiritual malady. And that's the basis of recovery—to develop that spirituality.

*The basis of recovery is developing
a new sense of spirituality.*

—Doc D., U.S. Army, 1968–1970

No Fight Club

I got stationed at a Navy air station in California. We got hauled in real late at night and early morning, and you could see the runway lights. Oh, it was beautiful.

The base also had Marines on it. They had their own barracks and their own bar. Navy personnel were not allowed in the Marine bar—unless you were female. My friend and I got to go into the bar, and we did our share of drinking. That Marine bar was the first place that somebody wanted to beat me up. I'm going, *Are you kidding me?* You know, I don't fight. I don't run away from a fight either. I should.

This girl just did not want to take no for an answer. And for whatever reason she called me a bitch and wanted to take me out in the parking lot. Well, she ended up walking away. I'm happy to say I never got into trouble for my drinking, but I probably should have.

Today the only fight I'm looking forward to
is the fight for my sanity in sobriety.

—Stephanie C., U.S. Navy, 1978–1983

Hope Is on the Horizon

I love seeing people cry when I tell my story—not just because it's my story, but because it reminds me that I'm alive. It reminds me that it's good now. It used to be bad, but it's not bad anymore. It's a reminder that today has to be better than yesterday, because yesterday is behind us. We have to make it better, not just for us, but for the people around us. That's how I want to be remembered.

So don't give up on yourself. You can make anything happen. You can be homeless and then buy a home. You can be addicted and then get into recovery.

Or you can die—and I don't mean a physical death. I mean a worse death: spiritual death. Then you can come to life again. We don't have tomorrow. We only have today.

Tomorrow is not promised, so I will choose to live in today, just for today.

—Armando S., U.S. Army, 2006–2009

Meditate, Meditate, Meditate

When I get up in the morning, I do my morning meditation. I've learned how to meditate. I do this for fifteen to thirty minutes every morning. It's part of my prayer meditation. I always read something. Mostly it's the basic texts and something out of my Bible.

I also do a ten o'clock meeting. As a part of NA, they have a Step Eleven Zoom meeting out of Las Vegas. Since COVID began, there are a lot of NA meetings online. Every morning they open it up with a couple of readings and a five-minute meditation. Then they have a speaker for fifteen minutes. They've been from all over the world. Then they open up for the last twenty minutes so people can share.

I also usually make a noon meeting on Monday, Wednesday, Friday, and Saturday. I am a meeting maker. I have a sponsor who has a sponsor, and I sponsor other people. I'm integrally involved in my recovery, because I truly believe this program works if you work it.

My routine in recovery keeps me focused,
centered, and on purpose.

—Karen A., U.S. Air National Guard, 1980–1991

My Past Is in the Past

Growing up, I dealt with life with drugs and alcohol. Initially, it was just to avoid the nightmares. I was already addicted to the life of drugs, but I was also addicted to avoiding my dreams.

I didn't know there was a way to deal with them in the military. At the time, all I knew was to deal with it on my own. Though my career was moving forward, I was still struggling with the bad dreams. Being prideful, I didn't reach out. Eventually, the military caught on to my usage, and there was an investigation.

I could have made different decisions. I wish things could have been different. I also wish I had reached out to somebody. That would have made such a difference. But I also believe that God put me through these things for a reason.

I can't change my past, but I can work on making a difference for my future.

—John F., U.S. Air Force, 1985–1996

"Progress, Not Perfection"

It took me years after getting discharged to finally get my life back on track. The guy I was living with was starting to get violent, so I ran away with my kids in the middle of the night.

I got sober in Killeen, Texas. I was totally broke, with no vehicle. This was right after Hurricane Katrina. Things were hard, but AA taught me that I could get my life back together again.

Recovery is a process, and it's been a long road for me. But my feet are planted firmly on it, and I'm headed in the right direction.

Today I'll remember that recovery is a process and sometimes you stumble. But as they say, it's about "Progress, not perfection."

—Warrior Priest, U.S. Navy, 1989–1995

AUGUST

Overcoming the Stigma of Recovery

When I told my mom I was going to go to a recovery meeting, she said, "Those people are crazy." She said, "I can't believe you're going to go to AA." I remember instantly being ashamed and embarrassed.

But I'm glad I did go. I remember thinking, *This is really cool to learn about drinking too much. And learn why I'm doing it. And, gee, I didn't notice that this behavior I exhibit goes along with my drinking.* I remember thinking it was interesting to hear people talk about things that I was doing and experiencing. Like, I wouldn't have known any of that if I hadn't gone to meetings.

I think the meetings are critical, because then you're also feeling some hope. You're hearing other people who are living like you do, but it's not out in the mainstream. You're thinking, *Oh, I sort of fit in here.*

For me, hope is the antidote to stigma. Because finding a place you belong helps you feel more at ease with your struggles and helps you feel like there may be a way to solve these problems.

Today I will work with others to bring hope into my life.

—Anonymous, U.S. Air Force, 1997–2000

Someone Cared

I felt something would go wrong if I told my company I needed help with my drinking—and it did. During my big drinking binge, I caused a bunch of trouble. It had been a few days since I had shown up for duty or anyone had seen me. They also hadn't come looking for me.

One day, the MPs grabbed me and brought me to my company area. While everybody started coming in for work, I just laid down on some chairs. Then my company commander came in and looked at me. I said, "I need help, sir." He replied, "Fuck you, man." Still drunk, I stood up and said, "Fuck you too, sir." Everybody in the room stopped, ready to jump me.

I eventually sought help on my own with civilian counselors and medical professionals. Afterward, the same people that were ready to jump me said, "Why didn't you come to me? I could have helped. You should have talked to me about it." I didn't know if I was going to be left behind again.

Since then, I've made a lot of progress not drinking and haven't had the same issues.

Speak up and speak out, no matter the circumstance. Someone will listen.

—Anonymous, U.S. Army, 2005–2009

Parallels between the Military and Recovery

Whenever I went outside the wire, I always knew that I had men to my left and right who were there fighting for me just as I was fighting for them. Down range, your unit's cohesion is the thing that will accomplish the mission and keep you alive.

Recovery is not much different. Some of the words that are ever-present in the rooms of recovery are the ones that echo the sentiment that you never have to go through this alone again. You have people to your left and right who will go out into the world with you and fight for you if need be. That cohesion will accomplish that mission. And it will most certainly keep you alive.

So be grateful for the team that you have on both these battlefields. It's a beautiful thing to know that you're not alone when life shows up and things get real. It's a godsend to have those people willing to fight for you just as you are a blessing to them for the very same reason.

Today I will make the conscious effort to be a present and active part of the team that might keep someone alive and bring them home safely.

—Bradley L., U.S. Army, 2005–2010

The Not-So-Subtle Presence of PTSD

I love my kids and see them as little creatures. They're amazing.

That said, with two deployments in Afghanistan under my belt, I had to meet my wife and kids—again.

When I came back home, suddenly, the wonder I once had for my children was gone. What I cared about was those little creatures doing what I needed them to do.

As in, *go to bed.*

If they didn't go, I would not-so-gently toss them into bed. *Go to sleep.* I just needed them to go to sleep.

I was making poor life choices.

I watched my relationships crumble.

I wasn't sleeping.

For somebody who has had a decent run of military service,

For somebody who came back from a couple of deployments and received some accolades,

For somebody who still hasn't had a sip of alcohol,

For somebody who is still in recovery . . .

The scariest part for me is, at least with alcohol, I can say, "My blood alcohol content is .20; that is abnormal." When it comes to mental health issues, it's like alcoholism except it isn't as tangible as blood levels.

Mental health is an intangible dis-ease.

—Matthew S., U.S. Navy, 2006–Currently Serving

Military Tools versus Sobriety Tools

The military taught me to anticipate problems, to react, and to solve problems. But with recovery, it wasn't a slam dunk. Getting sober is complicated.

I graduated from West Point. As time goes on, I've noticed that I'm not the only person from my alma mater who has struggled with addiction. There are many who have fought an arduous battle with alcohol or other substances.

Even though the military teaches us how to solve problems, addiction is often more difficult to solve and requires different tools than the ones we get from military training.

But there are always people around who have gotten this recovery thing. Instead of using military tools, we can look around us and get help from those who have gotten sober—who have gained new tools from living a life without alcohol. I needed help from someone who had been in the same addiction battle that I was in at that moment.

Reaching out to fellow addiction survivors
gives me the tools to embrace a sober life.

—Terry F., U.S. Army, 1986–1994

MISFIRE!

Struggling to adapt post-military led me down a dark and lonely road. I was trying to fit back into a society that just didn't make sense anymore. I was finally diagnosed with PTSD twenty-four years later.

I tried to drink myself better, but addiction doesn't fix anything. It hides the truth with false promises. I lost my friends and family, because I was no longer the same funny, charismatic guy. My life was in shambles. So I turned to hard-core drugs to escape. I can look back now to my Army days, serving in the Berlin Brigade and being proud of my service. Then I think of my ETS and college days and how the wheels came off my life because I was dealing with thoughts/emotions that I thought were not normal.

I've spent the better half of the last twenty years bouncing from the streets to prison and back, chasing something that was killing me. My story isn't special, because so many of us vets are dealing with the same issues, but what is special is how I found my military bearing and took back my life. After trying all types of treatment and therapies, I learned that my biggest strength was me.

I wake up each day trying to be a "better" person than before. I wake up ready to deal with whatever life deals me.

—JR W., U.S. Army, 1987–1995

Hope for the Future

My true friends? I don't have friends. I wrote a list of everyone I know, and the only people I can talk to are family, because I didn't use drugs with them. Everyone else in my life, I used drugs with. They weren't there to bail me out. They weren't there to answer my phone calls. But my dad answered the first time.

I hope my lowest point in my life starts to pave the road to my biggest success. Before sobriety I didn't know what I was doing. I was in the Army for six years and was told what to do every day. It's a big world out there.

Now I'm almost ninety days sober, and it's still scary not knowing what the fuck I am doing. I just hope to keep telling my story and help younger kids who are going down a shitty path.

"One day at a time" is my new daily mantra.

—Kory W., Canadian Armed Forces, 2009–2015

Humility

For alcoholics like me, humility is really hard. For me, it's like I'm either the best of the best or the worst of the worst—it's hard to stomach being in the middle. But God doesn't want me to live like I'm better than other people.

This is hard, especially being in the military, because you know they tell you that, out of all the people in America, only point-whatever percent actually are in the military. And of those, only this other tiny percent actually graduate boot camp and all that.

And so it really puts us on this high horse, and it's hard to get off that pedestal. It's tough.

Today I will remember that I am no better
or worse than anyone else, and I will focus
on remaining humble.

—Sean A., U.S. Army, 2007–2011

PTSD and Therapy

I was diagnosed with post-traumatic stress disorder. Fortunately I was sober and remained sober throughout my therapy for the PTSD. I did different therapies, and, all together, they worked.

One of my fears when I was having the PTSD dreams, nightmares, and flashbacks was losing those memories. I thought if I gave up those memories, if I didn't have those experiences anymore, I wouldn't feel anything. I didn't want to lose that, because it was like an old friend.

It took the therapist several times to tell me, "You're still going to have those feelings. They're just not going to be in the same spot in your brain, and they're not going to impact you the same way."

So now I still remember the dead. But they don't have the same effect on me that they used to. I can only thank therapy for that.

So I implore you fellow veterans—take the step. Do it. Just go exorcise those demons.

*Today I will seek help when I need it
in order to live the best life I can.*

—Ed C., U.S. Army, 1975–1979

I Will Use My Freedom Wisely

When I left the military and returned home, I had too much downtime. That is when I started drinking. At the time I believed drinking and partying was the best way to use my newfound freedom. But addiction is not freedom. Addiction controls us. We are powerless in its grasp.

Sobriety gives us the opportunity to find our own freedom. A truer version of freedom. Use this freedom to strengthen yourself physically, emotionally, and mentally. Use this freedom to serve your community. Use this time to connect with a purpose bigger than yourself.

You get to decide how to use your freedom.

Sobriety gives me the freedom I sought through my addiction. I am grateful for that freedom and will be mindful of how I use it every single day.

—Anonymous, U.S. Army, 2009–2016

Hang On to Your Tokens

It may sound corny, but when I got that first AA chip, I slept with it underneath my pillow—like I was waiting for the tooth fairy. Then, when I woke up in the morning, I would check for it and feel so good that it was still right there—that I was still there. I had a token to remind me that I didn't drink or black out the night before—that I had something to look forward to in the new day. I'd clutch it and say a little prayer: "Okay, let's do this."

I carried that "tangible token" in the pocket of my uniform when I was in the Navy. I took it everywhere. It got me through the in-between times when I didn't have the "intangible tokens" at hand—like the support and love of my group, or being able to talk to anyone about my feelings.

It was important for me to have something powerful to hold on to, something I could see and touch, something to remind me to take it "One day at a time."

Today I give thanks for my tangible and intangible tokens—the everyday reminders that, no matter what challenges arise, I can make it. I can do this.

—Elora K., U.S. Navy, 1997–2007

Daily Studies

I thoroughly enjoy recovery literature and have my whole reading routine in the morning. Some books I read once a month; some daily. *Around the Year with Emmett Fox* is more of a religious one. I'm also in a book study with my old sponsor on Tuesday nights, reading *The Untethered Soul*. We do other books, like *Drop the Rock*. It's a really good book about Steps Six and Seven of the Twelve Step program; that's what the whole book is about.

I read *As Bill Sees It*, my *Twelve Steps and Twelve Traditions*, the Big Book, and the *Al-Anon Service Manual*. I also have the Al-Anon *Blueprint for Progress*. It's over eighty pages long with a thorough three-page character checklist in the back: from "trustworthy" and "prone to gossip" to "envious" and "disagreeable."

How could I carry the message without the literature? It is an integral part of my recovery.

Reading recovery-based literature inspires
my daily stride in sobriety.

—Mary H., U.S. Navy, 1984–2004

Grateful for Recovery

I can connect the dots from when I had my first drunken blackout at nineteen until now. From that night on, alcohol was always a problem. I could never just have a drink and then go about the rest of my day. So as long as alcohol was in my life, I was never going to be as good a naval flight officer or as devoted a husband as I could have been sober.

Getting on the other side of active alcoholism and moving on to my life as a sober person has had many wonderful perks. My patient wife is much happier with me now. I'm now better able to reach my full potential in the Navy, because I didn't fully have my head together when I was drinking.

The other thing I didn't realize before I got sober is how many resources are available to individuals who are in recovery. Also, if you surround yourself with like-minded people who understand you, recovery will get a lot easier very quickly. I'm grateful for that too.

Today I will be grateful for the gifts of recovery.

—Guy C., U.S. Navy, 2005–Currently Serving

Finding Your Spiritual Way

Today I surround myself with my spiritual recovery people. Some live near me, and I'm also the veteran liaison at a farm that has equine-assisted psychotherapy. The farm's founder is also in recovery, so I always have somebody I can check in with if I'm having a hard day. I'm not doing it alone, and I have a spiritual depth I never had before.

I used to live in fear of getting drunk. But I found that if I live the spiritual principles, live a life of service, look honestly at my own mistakes, and make amends when I need to, I can live a good life. A sober life. And I'm living a good life now.

I also do meditation and I journal. And I ask my Higher Power for help when I need to. I'm not as impulsive as I used to be. If I don't know what to do, I'll wait for an answer. And if I screw up, I can find a way to own my side of it and move on.

At long last, my insides finally match my outsides.

Today I will not live in fear, because I know
I do not walk the recovery path alone.

—Deb L., U.S. Army, 1981–1996

Hope

Recovery was always in the back of my mind, but I had given up on the idea of being able to recover. I didn't know where help was, and I didn't know how to get it. No one offered it to me. I thought you had to have people who cared about you. I thought you needed people to personally reach out and get you help.

I didn't believe it at the time, but law enforcement was trying to help me. One of the officers had told me so at one of my arrests. He said, "We're going to get you the help you need today." I was just so mad at him. I was mad at the whole world. In reality, they were the ones who cared about me. Every time I caught another charge, I would get one step closer to being where I needed to be.

My probation officer was the one who finally did the intervention that I always wanted and needed. For that, I'm so grateful.

I have to be part of my recovery. God will help me move mountains, but I have to bring the shovel.

—Emil C., U.S. Navy, 1995–1997

Sharing My Story Helps Me Stay Sober

About five years ago, long after discharge and well into recovery, I had the honor of speaking to a lot of people at a recovery reunion. Telling my story helps keep me sober. And it's great to meet all these individuals who get it—they understand even though they didn't go through the exact same things. They've got similar struggles. Similar stories.

You get together with guys from all over the country and you talk about all the stuff you've experienced—your parents, your military time, whatever—all the insanity that we inflicted on ourselves and others when we were trying to numb ourselves with alcohol. The dishonesty, the craziness. The way we used people.

You hear it all the time: *stay connected, stay connected, stay connected.* And I do. If I'm having a bad day, I know I can pick up the phone and call any one of them and they'll be there for me. We'll talk for fifteen or twenty minutes. It helps, and that bad day is not as bad as it first seemed.

Today I'll connect with a friend in recovery
to thank them for being there for me and to
assure them I'm there for them too.

—Joe K., U.S. Coast Guard, 1988–1996

Learning to Love Ourselves

When I got kicked out of the military, I was like, *Oh my gosh. My life is over.* I took a picture of my uniform hanging on the door, thinking, *I'll never wear that again.* It messed me up.

My sponsor told me to come over. "I've got to get a job," I told her. "I need to do something. You know, have a sense of value." She asked if I got severance pay. I said yes. Then she said, "Why don't you just not work for a few months? Focus on your sobriety and your recovery program."

After nine and a half years in the military, knowing exactly what I had to do every moment of every day, the thought of doing nothing made my stomach turn. But I listened to her. I got to embrace the child within. I recalled the things I enjoyed doing. Bubble baths. Reading books. Listening to music. Having coffee and a cigarette on the beach. Just being still. I didn't realize how I hadn't been loving on me.

There's a saying in AA: "We'll love you until you learn to love yourself." And that is the absolute truth they were teaching me. And it was working.

> *Today I will slow down. Be still. And feel the love around and within me.*

—Elora K., U.S. Navy, 1997–2007

We're Not Alone

I can't even describe my amazement when I began reading the AA Big Book after I finally accepted that I'm an alcoholic. There I was, reading Bill W.'s story written in 1935, and it was my story. Everything said back in the 1930s fits me today. It meant I wasn't alone. The people in the book made it through, which meant maybe I could make it. It gave me hope.

Then, in the VA residence facility and afterward at meetings in the community, I found other veterans in recovery going through the same things I was. For years, I thought I was the only one who felt this way, then I discovered men and women vets who had been to the same places and who had the same inner struggles I had.

One of the biggest things in the military is that there's not one mission that gets done by itself. It's a team effort. You win together, and you lose together. Same for recovery.

No matter how difficult the journey may be, I now know that I do not travel the road to recovery alone.

—Kenneth B., U.S. Air Force, 2001–2007

Walking the Path Together

When my sponsor died after a heart transplant, I found another guy I really liked. He was a military warrant officer with about four years' sobriety. I barely had a year. We started going to daily meetings and did a formal Step study together—the best thing I've ever done.

We were best friends for thirty-four years, until he died. When I retired from the military, I went to work for the government and was able to hire him. We'd ride to work and have a meeting on the way. What a man. I used to tell him, "You know, every man is my teacher. Some teach me what to do. You've taught me a lot about what not to do."

He used to tell me, "You know, the deal works, but not all the dealers do. Not all the people in the program work the program." He worked the program each and every day. We knew everything about each other, and the hardest thing I ever had to do was to bury that sponsor after thirty-four years. But I'm so thankful that his lessons live on.

Today I treasure those friends, past and present,
I've met on the road to recovery.

—Mike F., U.S. Navy, 1959–1965/1972–1990

Spiritual Experience

When I was in treatment, I started listening to speaker meetings and identifying with the speakers. I thought, *Hey, they drank like I did.* I saw the similarities between us.

Then I found myself, this strong person who never cried, curled up in a ball in the middle of the floor surrounded by about twenty different people and a couple counselors. It was then that I said the same prayer that I think every single addict or alcoholic says at some point: "I don't know how to do this, and I don't know how to fix this. But, for crying out loud, if you even remotely exist, I could use your help right now, because I don't know what else to do."

I'm the same girl that spent her entire life trying to drink, drug, and fuck her way to some sort of unconditional love here on Earth. The first time in my life I felt that unconditional love was right there in the middle of that stupid room. I just felt warm and safe, and I had a belief that I'm going to be all right.

After that, the entire trajectory of my recovery changed.

Today I will be grateful for the spiritual experience that led me to recovery.

—Jenna R., U.S. Army, 2005–Currently Serving

A Higher Purpose

One of my friends from the National Guard invited me to join her in Alaska for the summer. I left Oregon, sold everything, and went up there for the summer. Here I had this brand-new bachelor's degree, and I ended up being her babysitter. It wasn't what I expected or needed at that time in my life.

So I went back to Oregon, got employment. I found that my services were needed in the Job Corps. I wasn't the person who did the program, but I was the person who took the kids to meetings. This form of service work for youth contributed to my sobriety both personally and professionally.

*Listening to others share their stories in sobriety
is a form of service work—for them, for me,
for all of us.*

—Gayle C., U.S. Army National Guard, 1976–1980/1984

Planting Seeds

Being a leader in the military is a lot like being a sponsor. If you take that responsibility to heart, you're helping people every day. It's not just with alcoholism—it's helping them to be a better person, worker, air traffic controller, parent, father, mother, whatever it is that you're helping them with.

If you're truly being a leader, it's rewarding. You invest in people. You don't do it for you; you do it for them. You're planting seeds. I planted a lot of seeds in my life, my career.

It's not often that you talk about your accomplishments in recovery, and they're so intertwined with the accomplishments of your profession. When you combine the two, they go hand in hand.

A rewarding role in leadership is rooted in recovery.

—Joe H., U.S. Navy, 1988–2015

My Takeaway and Excuse

Even before my first duty station, I showed up with a buddy, and we both must have smelled just like a brewery still. I think the drill sergeant made us do some push-ups and kind of laughed his head off and then, you know, told us to disappear.

I remember my takeaway from that was, *Okay, so that means we can get away with it. I can get away with this.* Even though the drinking age was twenty-one and I was still about eighteen, my alcohol use was laughed off instead of addressed head-on. I used that fact as an excuse to convince myself that it was all right to prioritize getting drunk over almost anything else.

> *On this day, I will stay accountable for my behavior and will not make excuses.*

—Dennis D., U.S. Army, 1997–2003

There Are No Coincidences

I've been sober forty-two years now and always had a sponsor, because as they say, "An alcoholic alone is in bad company."

I got my first sponsor out on the Indian Ocean. He was on my ship and had been sober about six months longer than me. I was finishing my Fourth Step inventory, and he suggested that when I got it all down, I should find someone else to hear my Fifth Step since he hadn't been sober that long. Fortunately, we had this Navy chaplain on the ship who had worked at a treatment center, and he agreed to hear it.

We stayed up for four hours talking about all the stuff I had done—the good, the bad, and the ugly. He cried. I cried. It was wonderful.

I went back to my bunk in my chief's quarters, and under my pillow found a copy of *Twenty-Four Hours a Day*, so I opened it to that day—June 30. It talked about living in the present and said not to carry the burden of past failures but to have faith that the clouds will clear and I can be made whole and free. That's when I learned there are no coincidences—God is everywhere.

Today I will update my personal inventory, because taking ongoing responsibility for my actions helps me stay sober and free.

—Bud N., U.S. Navy, 1957–1983

Alcohol Hurts Our Bodies

I'm a personal trainer, and when I studied for my fitness nutrition certification, there was a whole section on alcohol and what it does in the body. That education was really helpful to me, because I realized the truth about how I was harming myself. I think, culturally, we just pretend that alcohol is a fun vice that doesn't really hurt us. But actually, it can do a lot of damage.

That information helped me quit drinking—or at least, that's when the main struggle ended. I was just like, *Stop fighting reality.* I finally understood that I needed to stop drinking. I knew I wanted to get in shape and be healthy. Well, watching what you put in your mouth is one of the things that helps you get in shape. Consequently, I had to quit drinking alcohol.

Today I will remember that I deserve to be healthy and well, without putting destructive substances in my body.

—Eric S., U.S. Marine Corps, 2005–2009

You Are Not Alone

The great thing is that we don't have to do it alone. And that's probably the most important thing in recovery.

I have to admit that my way didn't work. It worked for a lot of years, over twenty-five years, but the last year of my using wasn't very effective. I wasn't getting the relief and the peace of mind—you know, I wasn't getting numb enough to satisfy my demons. So, if it wasn't working, we have to get honest and try something different.

And what I found was a way out.

I found people who were willing to show me how they did it. So we don't have to do it alone.

—Doc D., U.S. Army, 1968–1970

Two Lives in One

I'm surrounded by people in recovery. For eight and a half years now, I've lived this life that is so amazing. I've been given an opportunity to reengage in my sons' lives.

In 2020, right before COVID, I got married again. My wife is in recovery too. My oldest son is twenty-eight. My youngest is eighteen and will soon be my middle child, because my wife is currently pregnant with another boy. My wife is twenty-two years younger than me. She also has two kids that she did not raise because of what she went through with her family and addiction.

It's been challenging, but with those challenges come sunshine, hope, and the rainbows we see on TV and in our dreams. I love this way of life. I've been given an opportunity to live two lives in one lifetime.

Today I will see my second chance at life—
my second chance in recovery.

—Armando S., U.S. Army, 2006–2009

Rule 62: Don't Take Yourself So Damn Seriously

On bad days when I'm struggling, I pull a few coins out of my pocket that I've gathered over the years. These coins have phrases on them that remind me of key lessons I need to remember.

One of these coins has "Rule 62" on it.

Rule 62 is shorthand for an important reminder. It's the rule that says, "Don't take yourself so damn seriously." After all, sometimes the challenges we face on a daily basis seem like they are the worst thing in the world. But if I take a step back, and I remember that the most awful day in sobriety is better than sleeping on that step when I was homeless, then I can start to find the humor in what I'm going through today. I can get perspective and feel grateful for the life that God has given me.

My sober community helps too. I call them, and we laugh about what is going on in each other's lives. We keep each other grounded.

Just for today, I will keep things in perspective and not take myself so seriously.

—Dan N., U.S. Army, 1971–1977

Stay Connected

The last time I relapsed, my spouse was in the hospital. I went home alone and had to release the stress somehow. I went back to what I knew—drinking. I didn't reach out for support and came to the realization: connection was a big part that was missing.

When I tried to attend meetings and be of service to others, I was told I needed more time before I could partake in any real service positions. Since I wasn't getting connected, I started looking around for other support systems in sobriety. Beyond receiving text messages, reading my literature, and attending an AA meeting—if I needed in-person connection right away, I learned there were a lot of recovery programs online. With my online community, I've received so much support from others I haven't seen in person yet.

When in doubt, get plugged in with a community.

—Jen O., U.S. Army, 1995–2019

Accept Life as It Comes

Acceptance is a big part of my recovery. It's given me peace. When I don't accept things, I hold on to this perception of the *what if?*

Today when I accept whatever I encounter in life, I get this sense of joy and peace that I used to struggle to attain. I just accept life—what it is today. I don't boast about the gifts that I get back in my life. In sobriety, I get to see the good in my life. Sobriety means accepting life as it comes and being able to move forward in your day.

Today I'm very content. This is what my life has developed into.

Today I will move toward acceptance, peace, and joy.

—John F., U.S. Air Force, 1985–1996

Traveling in the Right Direction

After I got sober, I went back to Abilene, where I found that, if you were willing, there are a lot of different support programs available. Slowly, I signed up for programs for housing and other things I needed. Then I met somebody in recovery. He was from Detroit, and he was in Texas doing the same thing I was. We partnered up. We worked the program together, and eventually, he became my fiancé.

I was doing really well. But I was also trying to work on the sexual trauma I had experienced in the Navy, and that was really hard. I did a lot of backsliding before I had a really big mental breakdown. Fortunately, my fiancé was able to help me. I had given him power of attorney, and he was able to get me into a mental hospital.

It was a difficult time. He had to check me in three separate times over a six-month period. But they finally got me stabilized on medication. And my journey in recovery continued.

Just because you don't know your direction doesn't mean you don't have one. Today I trust that when I am lost in despair, God and fellow travelers will direct me.

—Warrior Priest, U.S. Navy, 1989–1995

SEPTEMBER

Alcoholism Exacerbates Stress; Use the Serenity Prayer Instead

Drinking exacerbated my stress. I didn't want to face how I was feeling, so I used substances to mask my discomfort. Alcoholism also stole my mental clarity. I couldn't focus and make a plan, which created more stress, which led to more drinking. Stuck in this cycle, I was not aware of how much I was hurting myself.

I was proud to serve my country. I was proud to have that opportunity. But let's face it: at the same time, service was anxiety-provoking.

Now that I'm sober, I address stressful situations using the Serenity Prayer:

> God, grant me the serenity
> to accept the things I cannot change,
> courage to change the things I can,
> and wisdom to know the difference.

When I was in the military, I felt like everything was so out of my control that I was just getting up and going through the motions like a robot. But that's really not true. I did have a choice about how I dealt with stress. Instead of using substances, I could have chosen a healthier way.

Today I will use healthier coping mechanisms rather than turning to substances for stress relief.

—Anonymous, U.S. Air Force, 1997–2000

Another Way

My unit never understood how difficult it was for me to stop drinking. They would assign someone to watch me sleep for weeks at a time—but I couldn't drink while I slept.

None of my peers or the leaders I talked to along the way to recovery were helpful in the sense of trying to fix the problem. High on the list of their priorities was telling me I had to get sober, return right back to my unit, that I was going to lose rank, get kicked out, or receive a dishonorable discharge. These are a few of the reasons why I kept running away and responding with a drink.

One day I sought help from civilian medical professionals. They told me there was a solution. I was relieved from constant uncertainty. They assured me I was not going to get kicked out as soon as I didn't have alcohol in my system.

No more running away. No more drinking.

Get help even when others don't understand or have an answer. Invest in yourself. Seek a solution.

—Anonymous, U.S. Army, 2005–2009

Finding My Way Back to Me

Combat and drug addiction erased the notion that I had any goodness left within me. I was irredeemable. I had not just burned bridges. I had roasted marshmallows over their flames. Because I felt like I was nothing but poison to the good people in my world.

I became a victim in my own story. So I put chemicals in my body to soften the edges. I continued until the edges were completely blunted and dull. I was a shadow of the person I used to be. I saw my brothers who I lost in combat as collateral damage to my self-destruction. And I was carrying their memories as excuses to keep poisoning my body.

So I made a decision to not use the memories of these people as a reason to keep killing myself. These were heroes. I became the best version of myself, because that's the only way I feel worthy of carrying their memory. Today they come with me everywhere, and I feel them working through me. That's the way it's supposed to be.

Today I will honor the people I loved and lost
by being the person they always knew me to be.

—Bradley L., U.S. Army, 2005–2010

Prayer Helps

I was stationed on the Navy's newest aircraft carrier, and there weren't a lot of people on it at the time. I was trying to find ways to stay sober while we were underway. That was a challenge. I leaned on prayer and meditation—mostly prayer.

As a new officer, overnight I went from being an E-5 to having an E-8 work for me. I was open with the personnel about my sobriety and the way I try to live my life. Simply out of survival, I knew I needed to have some level of honesty with other people, to let them know where I was at and what I was doing.

Practicing prayer and transparency
helps remove timidity in sobriety.

—Matthew S., U.S. Navy, 2006–Currently Serving

You Can't Outsource Recovery

You have to do the recovery thing yourself. You can't get anyone else to carry you through sobriety. This is just like in the military. You have to do your assigned job, look out for your unit, and take responsibility for yourself.

You don't want to be a burden on your unit. The thing is, when you get sober, you probably still have responsibilities too. Your job, your family, and everything else. But that doesn't mean you can't seek help from other people.

It's just that you can't expect someone else to get you sober. You have to do the work to get sober yourself, which means taking total responsibility for your recovery. What needs to change to make your life better? Make those changes!

It also means learning to stop beating yourself up. Learn to see recovery as a marathon and not a sprint. You need to focus on your recovery as much as possible, but you also have these other responsibilities, as we all do. Well, maybe you can get help. You should! But the one thing you can't offload is responsibility for yourself and your recovery.

Today I will take responsibility for my own recovery.

—Terry F., U.S. Army, 1986–1994

Don't Let the Past Ruin Today

When I was sobering up, I needed to be employed through a "work therapy" program. I was in a meeting with my counselor looking for jobs when I told her that I liked working at the VA hospital, so I wanted to get a job here. She looked at me like I had lost my mind. I am a convicted felon and would have to pass a background check. But I had accepted that my life was more valuable than what was on paper. I graduated drug court, and I showed up to work every day. I walked miles and rode buses to get there. I was on a mission to get hired at the VA medical center.

I realize the mountain I needed to climb to be considered for federal employment. I applied for the job, and my background was flagged. I called the background investigator and was honest about everything. He said that a housekeeping or kitchen position might be a better fit. I could have accepted that as a small victory, but it wasn't the position that I was training for. By the end of the call, he gave me a job in what I was trained to do, sterile processing. I just celebrated my second year of federal employment. Life changed when I started believing in myself again.

*Today I will live in the moment and
not let my past ruin today.*

—JR W., U.S. Army, 1987–1995

Grace Happens

I ruined every opportunity I had to get on my feet after being discharged from the service because of drugs. I'd sink into myself and become self-absorbed. Then I'd use drugs and just disappear. I was numb to the world.

I don't know how it happened, but about three years after I got hooked on meth, it seems like I became a drug dealer overnight. I think the amount of control you have over people when that happens is so powerful that it can become really evil. People start taking advantage of you, and eventually, you just say, *Fuck it.* You become hardened. You lose empathy.

I used things I learned in the military, like combat. I became really violent. I assaulted people. I broke into their homes. My own house was raided, and pretty soon I was broken and homeless. All I had was a bag of drugs and a criminal record. But by the grace of God, I didn't get thrown in prison. Veterans Treatment Court saved me.

Today I'll remember that shit happens.
But so does grace.

—Berlynn F., U.S. Marine Corps, 2009–2011

Unmanageability

I started smoking weed at fifteen and drinking at sixteen. I was kicked out of the military for my drug use. Everything I did just blew up in front of me and fell apart. All my best ideas ended up just sucking. It was easy for me to recognize that drugs and alcohol had made my life unmanageable. Sure.

Recognizing unmanageability was key in my life to getting sober. Because I had to acknowledge that I wasn't doing such a great job running my life. Maybe I could let someone else run it for a while. That someone else, to me, is my Higher Power.

Today I will recognize what is unmanageable in my life, and I will ask for help when I need it.

—Sean A., U.S. Army, 2007–2011

Monsters under the Bed

Until I gave my alcoholism a name, I was afraid of it. I didn't know what was going on. But here's an analogy: You're six, and you're afraid of the monsters that are under your bed. The reason you're afraid of them is because you can't identify what they are. You haven't confronted them. If you actually got out of your bed to look at them, you'd see that the monsters are really not that bad.

It's the same thing with alcohol. When I confronted my alcoholism, I recognized that *I am an alcoholic who is powerless over alcohol.* When I turned it over to my Higher Power, then my alcoholism didn't have the power it once did.

When you identify your enemy and make peace with it, it ceases to be your enemy. You can work with it.

So that's my message to you. There are those of us out here that root for you every day. And we'll see you in a meeting next time.

Today I will recognize that everything looks scarier in the dark, and I will be open to turning the light on.

—Ed C., U.S. Army, 1975–1979

Honesty Is My Key to Freedom

You can be extremely self-aware; that's great. But self-awareness will not stop you from losing yourself.

Why? Because we are often skilled at deceiving ourselves.

Secrets eat away at all of us and threaten our sobriety.

No matter how strong you are.

No matter how successful you are.

No matter how badass you think you might be.

You need to be honest with someone else about how you're really doing.

Honesty is what will set you free from the restraints of addiction.

Today I remember honesty will keep me humble.
Honesty will keep me connected to those I love.
Honesty is what makes the Steps work.
Honesty is my key to freedom.

—Anonymous, U.S. Army, 2009–2016

When the Training Kicks In

In the military, we're trained. We're overtrained. We do it once. We do it again. And again. We do it until we can do it in our sleep. We train until we can do it automatically, because we'll need it. We'll need it when we find ourselves in danger. And that's when "the training kicks in."

That's what the damn AA meetings are.

My dad never talked about being in the military;
he was in the service. And that's what this is.
Recovery is service.

—Don E., U.S. Army, 1967–1970

Rebuilding Trust

In my first years in the Navy, I'd only call my parents to tell about my accomplishments. They didn't know about my drinking problem. But when I got sent to restriction, they couldn't get hold of me to let me know my grandfather was hospitalized. I finally had to tell them.

They both got tired of all the ups and downs after that, so it took a long time for them to trust me again. But after my third duty station and two more alcohol-related incidents, I finally got sober and made amends. They've seen the results. They see how, with God's grace, I've grown.

Today is amazing. Now we celebrate my sobriety together. Now we can talk about everything.

*Today I am grateful that, in recovery, broken
relationships can be healed. Destroyed trust
can be rebuilt. Miracles can happen.*

—Elora K., U.S. Navy, 1997–2007

Sober Solutions

One of the very first times I had to share about my sobriety was at my first duty station when I was invited to a wedding. Beforehand, I went to an AA meeting and shared that I wanted to go. The people in the meeting said, "Drive your own car. Take a sober date. If you don't want to take a sober date, talk to the bride and groom, and tell them what's up." By then, though, pretty much everybody I worked with knew, because I'd been gone during the day for six weeks of day treatment.

By the time I got to my second duty station, my recovery wasn't something I would share just as I was checking in. Instead, I'd go to events and be like, "Hey, I can do the beer run, because I haven't been drinking." Eventually it wasn't something I hid.

If somebody needed company while attending their first meeting, I'd be available. There were also days I'd ask the boss if I could work an extra half hour to hit a meeting at lunchtime. Toward the very end of my military service, I didn't care who knew.

Today transparency serves as my sober solution.

—Mary H., U.S. Navy, 1984–2004

Vulnerability and Fear

It's not easy to be vulnerable right away. Whether you're scared because you don't want people to think you're weak or you are afraid of their judgment on the path you've taken, fear is what keeps most people from being honest.

But it's interesting. When you open up, it usually leads to everybody else opening up too. This happens because we all have the same anxiety that keeps our stories locked up behind our teeth. Realizing this means you don't have to be macho all the time. If you're around people who you can't open up with, maybe they're not the right people to be around. That's what I've found anyway.

It's gotten easier to be open with people as I've progressed in my sobriety. I don't need everyone to know my story, but I also don't need to be afraid of being "outed" for who I am. I'm becoming comfortable in my own skin. That takes practice and support, but it's a vital component of my sobriety path.

Just for today I will move away from fear and become more comfortable with vulnerability.

—Guy C., U.S. Navy, 2005–Currently Serving

Having Each Other's Backs

If someone in my recovery family is struggling, we immediately connect to form a circle of support. For example, when a friend—also a veteran—was suicidal, her therapist contacted all of us, asking if we would come in to be her support system. Our friend was able to see how much we loved and cared about her. We assured her we weren't there to "fix" her; we wanted her to know we had her back. It was truly deep.

We learn and grow together. We're doing a book study on nonviolent communication. Three of us veterans went on a retreat called "horse sense." We also walk by the river where I live and have campfires. During COVID, I started a women's meeting by the river. There's solid sobriety in the group. I have thirty-one years; some have even more. There's always someone to talk to about feelings—always someone to have my back.

We have traditions like carving pumpkins and making Christmas wreaths. We can be real with each other without having to fix each other. We can just be together and share how we're doing, and it's enough. It's everything.

Today I am secure in the knowledge that no matter what happens, my sisters in recovery will have my back.

—Deb L., U.S. Army, 1981–1996

Recovery and Healing

Recovery. No one offered it to me. I was just floating along in this dark sea of homelessness, drug use, and despair. It completely consumed me.

Not knowing what recovery looked like for me or how it was possible was really hard.

Through recovery and the healing process, I've been able to develop an identity for myself. I know who I am today. I stand for things, I have values, and I know that I'm resilient.

Today I will take advantage of whatever anybody has to offer me to benefit my recovery and healing.

—Emil C., U.S. Navy, 1995–1997

Creating Family

My dad was a great provider, but he was a physically and verbally abusive alcoholic. I don't know how my mom didn't kill him. I guess it's why she stayed out of the house so much with church-related activities and other things. I know it was why I joined the military. I never got involved in sports or anything as a kid, because if I failed, I was afraid I'd hear about it. By the time I was thirteen, my self-esteem was in the shitter. That's when my dad's drinking got to the blackout stages. He didn't know what he was doing.

He hasn't consumed alcohol for twenty-some years—he quit drinking about the time I left home. I was seventeen at the time. So the family joke for years has been, "Yeah, the day your dad quit drinking is the day you moved out."

I'm more selective about relationships these days. Those closest to me are friends in recovery or "normies" in my family. I call this group of people my "framily," because they are the family I've created.

Today I am thankful that in recovery we can create the family we wished for but never had.

—Joe K., U.S. Coast Guard, 1988–1996

Stop Drowning Myself

I know one of the reasons I started drinking was because of childhood trauma. At first, I was just being sociable as a teenager, trying to sneak beers. But then I discovered that feeling of numbness which provides a break from some of the thoughts—the bad thinking starts to go away for just a little while. I thoroughly enjoyed that experience of numbness and started to seek it out. That's how it all started for me.

But eventually, I just got to the point where I realized that the past, which occupied my mind in unpleasant ways, was out of my control and ultimately was never my fault. I can either continue to ruin my life by trying to drown myself and everything else with drugs and alcohol, or just try to push past it and do positive things instead.

Today I will focus on positive things
and leave the past behind me.

—John K., U.S. Navy, 2005–2009

Perseverance and Emotional Sobriety

Being sober in the military requires perseverance. Some days I don't have sobriety; I'm just dry. I'm pissed off, I am hot. It's 130 degrees, I'm wearing seventy pounds of battle rattle, and it feels like my brain is melting under this Kevlar.

I can't say in those moments that I'm feeling happy, joyous, and free. But what I do have is perseverance. The thing is, I know this is going to end. I know that I'm going to be able to get done with this tour; I know that I'm going to be able to get back to Minnesota where I'm going to freeze my ass off and have the polar opposite of 130 degrees Fahrenheit.

Today I will remember perseverance, which can carry us through when we don't have that emotional sobriety.

—J. D., U.S. Army, 1985–1993/1998–2018

Fighting Addiction Is Like Being in a Combat Zone

Getting sober was a key component in working on my mental health. I tried PTSD treatment at first, but I wasn't making any progress. If things got too overwhelming in therapy, I'd just get drunk. So I was just spinning my wheels until I started working on both issues at the same time.

The discipline I learned in the military really helped, because recovery is a very disciplined lifestyle. In basic training, you break things down into basic fundamentals. You wake up at a certain time, make your bed, go to PT . . . it's wash, rinse, repeat every day. Same for recovery. I've got to practice my Steps every day. Wash, rinse, repeat.

You need that structure in a combat zone. Fighting an addiction is sort of like being in a combat zone. You need structure there too.

I will continue to be as disciplined about my recovery as I had to be in basic training.

—Kenneth B., U.S. Air Force, 2001–2007

This Is Not a Game

Those of us who have been sober for a little while know that there is a percentage of alcoholics and drug users who aren't able to keep their sobriety. That is, a lot of people who get sober aren't able to stay sober.

I don't remember exactly what the numbers are, but they are disheartening. Looking at those odds scared the living hell out of me. It's like, *Wow, I better start listening to these people who have hung on to their sobriety, because this is not a game anymore.*

The challenge today is not about me trying to beat the cops or trying to get a judge to go easy on me or something. This is life-and-death stuff. For me, that's what keeps me coming back. Because I know how easily I can lose my sobriety and, therefore, my life.

Today I will remember how serious it is to stay sober, and I will take steps to hang on to my sober life.

—Mike D., U.S. Marine Corps, 1970–1974

Living by Design

I love AA. It saved my life. When I was in the military, I found I could go to meetings anyplace in the world—walk in and say, "Hi, my name is Mike, and I'm an alcoholic."

The program is designed for living, and if I live by that design, I live a good life. It works for me, because I want to be sober today more than I want to drink. And believe me, I wanted to drink every day.

The first ten years of my sobriety were in and out. I didn't drink, but I didn't surrender to God all the time. I came the closest I ever came to drinking again in 1994, when I was in a very sick relationship. Fortunately for me, I had friends in AA who dragged me aside and asked, "What the hell are you doing? Are you trying to get drunk? Because you're headed that way."

Thanks to them, I was able to end the toxic relationship and get back on the path to recovery where I belonged.

I will think of recovery as a verb—it is ongoing and fluid, something I practice every day.

—Mike F., U.S. Navy, 1959–1965/1972–1990

Two-Sided Coin

If you keep it really simple, you have two choices. In most of the situations that we put ourselves in, it's like a two-sided coin. On one side of the coin, there's fear. And on the other side, there's faith. It's really that simple.

A coin will not stand on its end. You just got to make a damn decision—decide which one you're going to choose. Then you're going to live with the decision you make. Every day you have to decide how you're going to proceed. Sometimes it's moment by moment.

As long as we can live on the side of faith, that's where we as alcoholics find freedom. When we find freedom in our own mind is when it allows us to be ultra-productive as human beings.

When my coin of life lands on fear, I will flip it over to the side of faith and choose freedom.

—Joe H., U.S. Navy, 1988–2015

Finding a Good Orderly Direction

When we got back to San Diego, my sponsor on my ship got transferred, so I asked this old ex–Hell's Angel biker named Motorcycle Don to sponsor me. He just died with forty-nine years of sobriety. The first thing he asked me was to define my Higher Power. When I couldn't, he said, "Well, if you don't find something greater than you, you're gonna die, and it ain't gonna be pretty."

I was walking through the woods and saw a bird's nest. That's when it hit me. If there are fertile eggs, all you have to do is keep them warm. They're not connected to anything, but that goo inside the egg turns into a bird with all this electrical energy inside its brain.

I went back and asked Don if my Higher Power could be whatever turns an egg into an eagle. I'm here to tell you if he had said no, I'd be dead today. But he said, "Hell, sounds good to me!"

I eventually got back to church and to God as I understood him as a kid. But I still tell newcomers it's okay if they don't believe in God; God still believes in them. Just don't drink, and keep coming back. Eventually, you'll believe in something.

On those days when I am filled with doubt and
despair, I have faith that my Higher Power
still walks with me.

—Bud N., U.S. Navy, 1957–1983

You're Stronger Than Your Vices

After all I've gone through to get sober, one of the things I now know is that you have to be stronger than your vices. When we're not in a good place mentally, we can start to depend on things that can harm us.

My advice to anyone who is still in that habit is, don't depend on what you think you need to depend on. You can push through those dependencies and make your life better. For example, I still encounter struggles every day. But now if I encounter an issue, I try to take a step back. If it's a life problem, I try to analyze the whole situation and figure out other solutions for it, rather than just getting mentally stuck and overwhelmed. Because if that happens, I could be tempted to reach out for one of my traditional coping mechanisms that aren't healthy for me.

Today I will remember the inner strength that can free me from unhealthy dependencies.

—Eric S., U.S. Marine Corps, 2005–2009

The Intervention by My Teenager

I remember one camping trip on a long holiday weekend. It rained the whole time, and my wife and I were getting drunk with the strangers and campers next to us. Our kids were being completely ignored.

A few days after that, our teen daughter confronted us with a family intervention. She told us her boundary was that if we didn't do something about our alcohol and drug use, she was going to move out and live with her brother. That got my attention. I agreed to go talk to a treatment center. The only promise I made was that I would keep an open mind. I had no plans to quit drinking. No plans to quit using pot. But I said I would keep an open mind. And I think that's the thing that saved me.

And all of a sudden, I was going four days a week, four hours a day to an intensive outpatient treatment center.

Keeping an open mind is the thing that saved me.

—Doc D., U.S. Army, 1968–1970

Tag Team

Some people get ten feet tall when they drink. When I got drunk, I grew five inches taller. I was gorgeous. I was beautiful. I had a personality that wouldn't stop. I was all that and then some.

When I wasn't drinking, I was five foot three, quiet and hurt. I had that sore heart. It's because of the sore that I drank—to stop the pain. All I wanted was for it to stop, so I got help and started attending AA.

Now my twin sister and I have the same amount of time in recovery. She said if I could do it, she could do it. We kind of tag-teamed each other. But she still had to do her recovery work, and I did mine.

Today I remove the heart sore with healing and love rather than a drink or a drug.

—Stephanie C., U.S. Navy, 1978–1983

I Am an Agent of Change

After the military I became a fully engaged service member within Narcotics Anonymous. A social worker asked me, "Why don't you become a social worker?" This introduced me to the whole world of getting educated. I got an associate's at San Antonio College, got a bachelor's in social work from Our Lady of the Lake University, and I graduated with my master's in social work from the University of Texas.

I became a social worker and started seeing the other side of it. I started seeing how we can bridge gaps by learning and teaching others to communicate—to talk, love, share. These things can change the world.

This work just became a part of me. Today I am an agent of change and I'm going to spend the rest of my life doing this.

Today I will serve as an agent of change—touching lives in my community and touching lives worldwide.

—Armando S., U.S. Army, 2006–2009

Waiting Season

Today my husband and I are both veterans, and we're recovering together. It wasn't always this way. It took me doing some work on me and taking a hiatus from dating. My picker was broken. I was picking the wrong ones, and that was the problem—I would do the picking. I had to take a break. I let go and was like, *You know what, God? I'm taking a break. You pick the next one. I'm leaving this in your hands. Your will be done. You know what's best for me.*

I stepped away from dating, from talking to anyone, from doing anything for a year and a half. A year and a half—nothing. My family was like, "You're not dating?" I would say, "Oh, no, no, no, no, no. I'm waiting. I'm in a waiting season. I'll know when it's time when God's ready for me to have someone. It'll come."

And then one day I was sitting in a meeting and my future husband tapped me on the shoulder and asked me for a reading. And we started laughing with each other. We've been together since then. And that's all she wrote. We've been together since then.

In his perfect timing, God supplies my needs rather than my wants.

—Karen A., U.S. Air National Guard, 1980–1991

It Takes Time

It took me twenty years to get it. You know what they say: "You can lead a horse to water, but you can't make it drink."

Even so, I think exposure to recovery and the feeling of conviction you get from somebody that you're learning from have a lot to do with it. They plant the seed, nurture it, let it grow. That's what recovery is about for me. It's not something that you just walk into a store and pick up off the shelf and say, "I got some recovery."

My recovery is homegrown. It took years to take hold of. Today I get to water my recovery every day.

Water and nurture your recovery
with passion every day.

—John F., U.S. Air Force, 1985–1996

OCTOBER

Me and God Didn't Get Along

When I started thinking that maybe I wanted to get sober, someone told me I needed to turn my life over to God. I said, "That's not for me, thanks. Me and God don't get along. He don't like me, and I don't like him. I told him to get lost and he said the same thing to me."

Well, they told me if I didn't want to pray this prayer, to do this thing, well, then there was the door, so good luck on my own. So I said, "All right, I'll do it." I went out and I said, "All right. God, this is the way it is. I have screwed up my life. We can both agree on that. If you think you can do better, be my guest."

Well, that was the start of something big. I've never regretted that prayer. It's helped me stay away from alcohol. I just get out of the way and let God work.

Today I will recognize that I can't do it all by myself,
and I will be open to a different path.

—Dan N., U.S. Army, 1971–1977

What Are Your Priorities?

If there was anything I could go back and ask myself when I was using, it would be, "What are your priorities?" Back then I didn't think broadly about what my life was and what I was doing. For my quality of life and overall well-being, I wish I had asked myself, "What is important to you?"

My priorities should have been my kids first and then the military. If I had asked myself this question, then maybe I would have said, *Well, geez, if those are my priorities, what can I do to facilitate my relationship with my kids and be the best mom I can be?*

Maybe if I had asked myself this question, I would have thought about the fact that I was leaving my kids with my mom or my in-laws during leave time so that I could go out and drink. Maybe I wouldn't have done that, but I don't know. I can't go back in time. All I know is that, now, I work on getting my priorities straight.

Today I will ask myself, "What are your priorities?"

—Anonymous, U.S. Air Force, 1997–2000

Hope Is on the Horizon

Open to whatever, I didn't think it was a big deal to be young in a combat zone. I wasn't around people drinking, but there were people abusing drugs within my unit. Some people dealt with our environment by abusing a substance—whatever they could get ahold of—or just bottling it up. We weren't really given any care while there or when we got home.

There's a system, then there are individuals operating within the system. When I was having issues with drinking and brought it to the attention of the wrong person, it made things worse.

As an alternative, I attended outpatient counseling every day. I learned I wasn't the only person with an alcohol problem. We shared a common thread of hope.

It may feel like you're alone, but you're not.

—Anonymous, U.S. Army, 2005–2009

Knowing God Is Better Than Playing God

Whether as a heroin addict or an infantry soldier, I wielded the same power over life. The only difference is that as a soldier, I decided the fate of any person who was unlucky enough to be in my sight. As a heroin addict, I had the choice as to whether my life was worth living.

Today I find myself humbled and grateful in my relationship with God. Praying to him felt so strange at first. Now it feels like we are having a personal conversation. I see him in daily miracles. For me, it was going twenty-four hours without putting something in my body that made me feel any way other than normal.

My motivations are not the same as they were before. Intentions that were once self-serving and prideful have become lessons in humility and selflessness. I used to ask for so many inconsequential things in prayer.

Today I pray for everyone else and ask that God gives me the clarity to know his will and the courage to allow it to direct my steps.

Today I will make a point to ask God to show me his will. Today God will direct my every step, no matter how small.

—Bradley L., U.S. Army, 2005–2010

Tough Times, Tougher Recovery Program

I spent nine months in western Afghanistan, working directly with the Afghans. I spent a lot of time outside the wire—which means you're out in the shit. It wasn't exactly the friendliest environment.

There was a kid on base drinking quite a bit. I knew it, but I didn't write him out to the chain of command. Instead, I worked with him. I had my Big Book, talked to him about it; we worked through stuff and tried to find ways to stay sober.

While serving in Afghanistan, I took my five-year chip during a Zoom meeting with my home group back in Suffolk, Virginia. While on R & R, I went to a meeting in Kandahar and got another five-year sobriety coin. For me it was a crazy time—I got blown up, we got chased out of buildings, and I built a solid relationship with an interpreter. Sobriety underpinned all of that.

The biggest takeaway? When my ass is on fire, I get back to the basics. If I do that, things tend to work out.

I wouldn't have survived without being in recovery and trying to stay connected to it.

My program of recovery follows me wherever
I go—domestic and foreign lands.

—Matthew S., U.S. Navy, 2006–Currently Serving

There Is More

My recovery was not a linear journey. I was first introduced to recovery in the late nineties, when I was active duty in the military. Almost two years ago, just before the pandemic, I got sick of waking up and not feeling happy. All I could think was, *There has to be more to life than this.* And drinking just wasn't it. It wasn't fun anymore.

To paraphrase a term I've heard in the rooms of AA, I got sick and tired of being sick and tired. There was an overwhelming feeling. There has to be more to life than this.

In time, I took the leap. I became willing to seek recovery for myself. Thankfully, this time around, I stuck with it.

There is more to life when we choose recovery.

—Jen O., U.S. Army, 1995–2019

Find Your People

I believe that connection is the opposite of addiction. We have to have these bonds with other sober veterans like us. For me, that's the only thing that really pulled me out. The more programs that we have for recovery, the better! Because these programs help you find your people.

I don't know where I would be if it wasn't for the fellow vets at the hospital. I mean, these guys, they've seen me grow into the person I am today.

The sobriety program doesn't have to be AA. Nowadays there are so many options for meeting other sober veterans. I encourage everyone to be open to building community—it is my best strategy for letting go of hopelessness and addiction.

Today I will look for opportunities to connect with other soldiers and veterans in recovery.

—JR W., U.S. Army, 1987–1995

Loving the Unlovable

I got out of the Marines with a general discharge under honorable conditions. So I was out, and my paycheck was gone. I had an apartment and a vehicle—things I didn't know how to manage in the first place, so I ended up losing it all. I just bounced around from state to state. I couldn't manage anything. I didn't know how to communicate my needs or deal with my problems. I burned bridges and just ran away.

I ended up back in my hometown in California, where I was introduced to meth. Meth was just like bath salts, only I didn't lose my mind. Or so I thought.

My stepbrother's mom took me in and just gave me everything, but I destroyed that. Luckily, because of my recovery program, we were able to rebuild our relationship. Now having the clarity to look back, so many people were offering me love. I just didn't see it, because I didn't really know what real love looked like back then.

When your primary relationship is with drugs, there's no room for anyone or anything else.

Today I am grateful for those who loved me,
even during my most unlovable times.

—Berlynn F., U.S. Marine Corps, 2009–2011

I'm the Man I Always Wished I Could Be

A friend reminded me once, "You're the man you always wished you could be." I thought about it, and damn, she was right.

But I didn't get there by myself. In recovery, I had to ask people for help—I had to be willing to continue asking for help, because that's the only reason why I'm sober. That's a lesson that I learned.

My internal wiring has changed through recovery. My old wiring would say, *I've got this! I've figured it out myself.* My new internal wiring tells me I need to call someone, I need help, I can't do this alone.

I can look back from the phone call to a caseworker that got me into treatment all the way to today, when I had a job offer and I called someone to learn how to negotiate. I am not doing this all by myself, and I'm so grateful for that!

On this day, I will be thankful for those who have helped me become the person I am today.

—Sean A., U.S. Army, 2007–2011

Seek Out Accountability

You already know the power of accountability. You know what it's like to have someone watching your back while you watch theirs. You know how it feels to show up for something bigger than yourself. Depending on how much time you've spent in the civilian world since, you know how aimless it can feel to be without it.

This journey is a tough one, but there is strength in numbers. Go to your meetings. Call your sponsor. Connect with the community. Seek out the accountability you need to stay the course.

*Today I will remember that I do not need to travel
down this path alone. I will seek the accountability
I need to support myself while also supporting
someone else on their journey.*

—Anonymous, U.S. Army, 2009–2016

Miracles Happen

When I received my fourth alcohol-related incident, I knew my military career was over. Career aside, it was the first time I was scared for my life. Our division officer had just checked in to our command. When the lead introduced the crew in the radar room, the new lieutenant turned to me, said my last name, and stated, "I heard about you." Then he asked me to visit him in his office for a talk.

Within minutes, he had recited my drinking history and told me that I was on the road to spiritual destruction and I needed to look beyond self—the type of language I had only heard at AA. Then he said, "We don't know each other, but I'm a friend of Bill W." I just cried. He proceeded to use a coin analogy to describe making choices in fear and faith, and told me, "Go to ninety meetings in ninety days, and my door is always open."

I committed to meetings and knocked on his door when needed. It was like the two of us had mini meetings. I did that for a month and a half until I got discharged. I felt different, because I had a willingness and someone to say "You can do this." Fourteen years later, I'm still sober because of people like him.

Today I will remember that help is there when I need it.
I only have to be willing to open the door.

—Elora K., U.S. Navy, 1997–2007

Aha Moments

Every Sunday morning there's over a hundred people attending an AA meeting down the street from my house on the beach. There's a two-story building on the water down there, where you get to see "drunks" coming for seven, noon, five-thirty, and nighttime meetings. We've moved the noon meeting outside to the park, because we're still pandemic afraid.

One day a million-dollar yacht pulled up. The dude came straight to the meeting. Can you imagine? All walks of life.

One day a boat called *Happy Trails* appeared; *Moments of Grace* parked next to it. Then *Happy Destiny* moved in when *Happy Trails* left. No kidding. I kid you not. It was really cool! Is that a coincidence? I don't think so. We know and understand these aha moments nowadays, because we're sober enough to pay attention.

We receive messages of hope daily from unlikely places. Today I am willing to acknowledge them with gratitude whenever they cross my path.

—Mary H., U.S. Navy, 1984–2004

Defining "Rock Bottom"

Everybody defines their rock bottom differently. If you're not done, it's going to be hard to do what it takes to walk the sober path. As they say, if you try sobriety and you don't like it, you can always go back out: we'll refund your misery for free.

You have got to be honest with yourself and everybody around you, and you have to want sobriety for yourself. You can't do it because your wife tells you to get sober or your boss wants you to quit. I tried to get sober for other people. It didn't work.

I was only able to stay sober when I wanted it for myself. Eventually, I was crying on my way to work, because I was scared of not drinking. I finally knew I was done. Only then was I able to walk forward in sobriety.

On this day, I will remember my own "rock bottom" and the reasons I don't want to go back there again.

—Guy C., U.S. Navy, 2005–Currently Serving

Flying Sober

Recovery is so much more than sitting in a meeting room. I view sobriety and meetings as a bridge that takes us into our life beyond them, to where we can practice the spiritual principles and embrace the program in what we do every day. I practice gratitude and try to show my appreciation for the people and things around me.

I got sober when I joined the Guard after active duty. I had to take a flight with some officers, and I had never flown sober before. So I found the chaplain in our unit and sat next to him, clutching my Big Book and talking about AA.

There was a lot of partying going on in the National Guard, but I managed to seek out sober friends and find meetings when I needed to. That's how it's been since I decided to get sober. My Higher Power put people in my life right when I needed them, and said, "Pay attention. Take action." The longer you're in the program, the more friends you have all over the place.

Today I will show my gratitude to those around me who support my recovery and to my Higher Power for guiding me to them.

—Deb L., U.S. Army, 1981–1996

Be Your Own Advocate

I was able to put down all the drugs. The hardest part was putting down the opioids. After twenty years of opioid use, it wasn't so simple as to just put them down and white-knuckle it through.

I was abstinent for six months. I was off of all drugs, but I felt worse than ever. I was suicidal and I didn't know how long I would be able to maintain my recovery without additional help. My recovery required medication.

One of the hardest things I've had to do since I got clean was stand in front of a whole team of people in the courtroom. This included the judge and all the people who were there with different opposing opinions about medication-assisted treatment and what that looks like to them—what they think versus what the science says. I knew in my heart that I didn't want to abuse the medication I needed in order to feel human again. I had written the judge a letter. It was an emotional time for me as I stood there in front of all those people who were accusing me of trying to manipulate the system.

The judge granted me an opportunity. I could barely hear the words. Man, from that moment forward, I've never looked back.

Today and every day, I find my voice to speak
my truth and advocate for myself and my recovery.
Leave no one behind—including me.

—Emil C., U.S. Navy, 1995–1997

Surviving and Thriving

A lot of guys like me, who were abused, are no longer with us. Some drank themselves to death or committed suicide in other ways. I'm still here, one day at a time.

I still struggle a lot, but I know that going back to using isn't the answer—just like joining the military wasn't the answer. That's why I stay connected with others in recovery. It's why I do service work. Sometimes it feels easier to help others than to help myself.

A girl I had known for a long time came back into my life—possibly because she knew I was in recovery. She had gotten her second DUI and broke down and told me, "I don't want to do this anymore. I need help." So we made a call to her employee assistance program at her work, and she got into a women's treatment program. Now we live together in a beautiful coastal home as life partners—drug and alcohol free!

Living with someone who is also in recovery can be challenging. I have ADHD, so I'm not as present as I want to be. She knows about recovery and trauma, so she understands. We talk, and we keep learning. It gives us something to work on tomorrow!

Today I'll practice being present with others.
Today I'll reach out, be still, listen, and learn.

—Joe K., U.S. Coast Guard, 1988–1996

Relapse

Relapse is a part of my story. I certainly stumbled a few times. I've relapsed twice since I got out of the hospital. Both times, my relapses were pretty bad situations. But, luckily, I was able to come back within a week or two both times. I'm grateful for that.

What helped me each time was realizing that I was just heading down that same path again and knowing I had to pull out of it, because I didn't want to get to the point where I was hospitalized again. Hospitalization had shown me how bad it can get out there, and I didn't want to get to that point again.

I work full time now at my own business, and I am pretty stable for the most part. I think a lot of that is due to weekly therapy and group sessions. Instead of the routine where drugs are a part of my everyday life, I have a sobriety routine. That helps a lot.

Today I will recognize that relapses happen,
but getting into a sober routine with others
can stave off backslides.

—John K., U.S. Navy, 2005–2009

Formula for Success

Everyone has a different formula for success in recovery. What's important is to not forget what has made you successful in the past. Don't let go of your formula, because we are vulnerable when we don't have a good routine to keep us sober.

Something I've seen in both the military and recovery is someone who has a successful formula for taking care of their life, which requires discipline, requires them to be connected, and requires them to be honest and faithful. At some point, these people may convince themselves that they don't have to do those things anymore. Well, that's where the trouble starts.

I have forty-plus years of sobriety, and I follow the same formula from when I got sober at fifteen: put as much energy into recovery as you did into getting drunk or high.

Today I will remember my formula for success and will hold tight to what keeps me successful.

—J. D., U.S. Army, 1985–1993/1998–2018

Getting out of My Own Way

In early recovery, I tried to buck the system. I was a pain in the butt, until a peer supporter said, "You can stay as sick as you want for as long as you want, and there's no one to stop you, except for you. If you leave here with the attitude of 'I know everything,' you're gonna end up drinking, and probably end up killing yourself. The decision is up to you."

I needed that reality check, and it was eye opening. I didn't want to stay sick, and I realized I couldn't get better unless I took the necessary steps. Everything changed after that. When you begin recovery, you hear "Ninety meetings in ninety days." I blew that stat out of the water. I was probably hitting three to four meetings a day. I wouldn't talk. I'd just listen—that went back to my military training. Nobody was going to recover for me. I needed to dig in and do the work myself.

When it comes to recovery, we can be our own worst enemies. I'll continue to get out of my own way and trust the process. "It works, if you work it."

—Kenneth B., U.S. Air Force, 2001–2007

Family Consequences

My daughter was noticeably impacted by my drinking. She developed some anger at me for more or less emotionally abandoning her for all those years. One of the ways she coped with my drinking was to try and fix me.

I'd be passed out on the couch, and she would go into the trash can and get all the empty beer cans, and lay them on my chest and spread them out. So when I came to, or woke up, beer cans would go flying.

That was her way of saying, *Hey, go quit this shit.*

But thankfully, she's been supportive of me in recovery. That's another thing I have to be grateful for.

Today I will remember the past without regret, because I have made changes to stay sober today.

—Mike D., U.S. Marine Corps, 1970–1974

Second Chances

I have a daughter that I didn't meet until she was twenty-three years old, when I was stationed in San Diego. Her mother had told her she would help her find me. They went to my sister's house and, through her, got my address.

And so she sent me a letter saying, "Dear Dad, bet you never thought you'd hear from me." She went on to say that I was the missing link in her life and that she wanted to get to know me. At the end, she wrote, "If you got any balls, call me." Before I called her, I called my sister, saying I wasn't sure this young woman was my daughter. My sister cracked up, saying, "There's no doubt. She looks just like you."

We have a great relationship now, and she's even my caretaker if anything happens to me. Because I'm sober, I've been able to make amends to her and to all my children. Plus I have twenty-four grandchildren and great-grandchildren and two more on the way. I'm a lucky man. God does amazing things.

*Today I am thankful for second chances and
all the gifts that recovery has given.*

—Mike F., U.S. Navy, 1959–1965/1972–1990

God's Will versus Being Willing

That God part is not easy for any of us. For me, it was a process. I remember taking that damn Third Step. Trying to make it something that it wasn't, trying to be a perfectionist, I said, "How do I know when I've surrendered? How do I know I'm doing God's will?"

My sponsor very eloquently told me, "It doesn't say that you're doing God's will. It says you're willing!"

It hit me like a ton of bricks. I was overcomplicating this.

Getting on board with a Higher Power is obviously a big point in anybody's sobriety. Because if you don't have that, you can't move on, because the fear gets in your way.

Today I will focus on my willingness
rather than doing God's will.

—Joe H., U.S. Navy, 1988–2015

Recovery Improved My Mental Health

Recovery is so much better than I could have possibly imagined. When I first started looking at recovery, I was extremely scared. I did not believe it was possible to stay sober for the long term—certainly not for me.

Now my mental health is so much better, and my moods are on an even keel. The lows aren't as low, and the extremes are not as extreme. Before I got sober, a lot of my life was ruled by emotions. I'm thankful to say that's not as prevalent today. Emotions don't control me as much as they used to.

I've been able to sit back and listen. I take a second, evaluate something, and think about it before I act on it. I almost never did that when I was drinking and using. Back then, I would just act without thinking half the time. I feel like I've been given a second chance.

*Today I will remember that recovery
has given me a second chance at life.*

—Dennis D., U.S. Army, 1997–2003

Living in the Mystery

I'm remarried to a wonderful woman who is also in AA. I have a good relationship with my kids now and made amends to all of them. I was a master chief, and my son retired as E-9 master chief, and my grandson is going up for chief. I pray for my other son, but I know I can't fix him.

My daughter "Fluff" was also in AA. She was forty-six when she called to say, "I have stage IV cancer. Can I stay with you?" We put up a hospital bed, got hospice, and a woman from AA came to do meetings. When we moved her to her son's after he got home from Afghanistan, I asked her to send me a sign to let me know she was all right.

Six weeks later, my wife and I got back from running errands to discover a card on the Jeep window that simply said, "Everything's gonna be okay." I tucked it in my pocket, and we went to have tea outside. That's when a beautiful butterfly landed in my wife's hair. We looked at the time, and at that exact moment, Fluff's son called to say she had died.

Fluff always believed butterflies were angels. And now I do too.

Today I will pay attention and live in the mystery,
and thank God for the many gifts he continues
to send my way.

—Bud N., U.S. Navy, 1957–1983

No One Can Do This for You

One of my friends that I grew up with has gotten two or three DUIs now. I talk to his mom all the time, because she lives near my parents.

As much as I'd like to help my friend get better, I can't hand the keys to sobriety over to him. As I told his mom, it's on him. He has to want to do it. We can sit here and talk to him until we're blue in the face. But it's up to him to say, "I want to get better." Because we all need that inner strength to get past our vices. No one else can give that strength to you. But we can help each other along the way.

People ask me what's worked for me, and I'm happy to pass on my experience. I've mainly used meditation and therapy to help me get sober—along with educating myself on what alcohol does to the physical body.

Every person needs to take responsibility for their own recovery. That's the only way to make it stick on a long-term basis.

Today I will take responsibility for
maintaining my own sobriety.

—Eric S., U.S. Marine Corps, 2005–2009

Fellowship Is Power

You know, every day when I leave the house, I carry two coins with me. That's my twenty-eight-year coin and the Vietnam Vet in Recovery one, which my counselor gave me. I've carried it in my pocket every day for over twenty-five years. I never leave home without those in my pocket.

Early in recovery, I would reach in my pocket whenever I had a temptation or craving, and I'd hang on tight to that thing and say the Serenity Prayer: "God, grant me the serenity to accept the things I cannot change, courage to change the things I can, and wisdom to know the difference." Because I had no power.

Sponsorship is a great thing. My sponsor has thirty-three years. And I know my sponsor's sponsor, who is a Vietnam veteran with thirty-six years. The fellowship book tells us that fellowship is a sufficient substitute for alcohol. And I hang on. I hang out with the winners. Pretty simple.

Today I will remember to hang tight to my coins,
talk to my sponsor, and know fellowship
is important.

—Doc D., U.S. Army, 1968–1970

Getting to Know Me

Several years after serving in the Navy, I began attending AA meetings. I went two or three times a day. I felt at home. I felt wanted, loved, welcomed, and accepted for who I was. I didn't have to pretend to be anything or anyone. I could be Stephanie.

Now, the hard part about this was that I didn't know who I was, and that scared me. In the meetings they told me once I got rid of the booze and stuff, then I would start growing. That scared me even worse. So I'm doing the work, and the Ninth Step promises tell me, "You're going to come to know a new this and a new that" and a bunch of stuff.

I thought, *What if I do all that work, and I don't like who I am?* I despised myself for years, and now the recovery community was telling me I was going to get clean and sober. I have to say, after all that work and stuff, I'm still not six feet tall. My legs are just as close to the ground as they were when I was drinking, but I have a happiness and a joy I never knew growing up.

Part of my happiness and joy comes from getting to learn who I am in recovery.

—Stephanie C., U.S. Navy, 1978–1983

No More Secrets

We keep secrets. I think it's one of those things that we do in the Black community. We keep family secrets from a long time ago. They're passed down to us in our childhood. They used to always say, "Don't say nothing." And some people wonder why we are addicts.

We have to learn how to unlearn keeping secrets, because secrets keep us sick. We're out here not talking about stuff, because we're used to not talking. I've learned so much about ancestry, about unearthing these dark secrets that have kept us sick in my family.

That's a struggle. We have to let go of the stigma that says because we're Black we can't talk about what's going on. Nobody can help you unless you let somebody know.

Today I will break the generational cycle and shed light on the secrets that haunted me in my addiction. Today I will heal in my recovery.

—Karen A., U.S. Air National Guard, 1980–1991

We Are Worthy

I never realized how ashamed I was of my active using until I began judging my self-worth based off how many days I had clean. The more years I had under my belt, the better I thought I was. Eventually I began to stigmatize the very population I sought out to help—those still struggling with active using.

I became certified as a peer support specialist and painfully realized I lacked compassion and empathy for others because I lacked it for myself. Even more so, I began to understand and believe I am worth just as much on my worst day of using than I am today with four-plus years (I stopped counting).

I am worthy of love, tolerance, respect, and kindness. We are worthy.

Today I will reach out and support someone still struggling with active use.

—Berlynn F., U.S. Marine Corps, 2009–2011

The Power of Prayer

Early on in my recovery, I met a guy in AA who was on a parallel path, and we ended up together. He had gotten sober with a Christian biker group, and his spirituality was based on service. He helped me through some really hard times.

He was my best friend, and after a few years, we got married. But then, a short time later, he passed away from throat cancer. I was alone, facing not only addiction and recovery, but also bereavement over losing my best friend. In my isolation, I really started reaching out to God. I'd watch all these TV evangelists, and I learned how to pray. What I learned from prayer was that my problems wouldn't always go away, but I would have the strength to walk through them.

I also got very involved with AA, both at the district and area levels. I realized that service is what keeps you focused on your recovery. I became more of a warrior for recovery based on service.

Today I'll remember that grief is a heavy burden to bear, but it is made lighter by praying, working my program, and helping others.

—Warrior Priest, U.S. Navy, 1989–1995

Today Is a New Day

There are moments of struggle daily. I used to put in so much of a fight every day to get the drugs. I have to put that same effort into not using, or I have to double that effort.

It's very easy to quit. Quitting is easier than succeeding. Put it that way, and I can't quit. I have to succeed. It's in my blood. It's the way I'm wired. I'm competitive. Not for anyone's sake but my own.

Less than ninety days sober; that's where I'm at right now.

No matter my time in recovery,
my effort into today is my priority.

—Kory W., Canadian Armed Forces, 2009–2015

NOVEMBER

Military Sacrifice

Civilians are not aware of the sacrifices made by military members. I underestimated the stress I would be under while I was serving. For my fellow service members, it is extraordinary that you're all doing this—that you've all done this. Because once I joined, I felt there was a huge disconnect between civilian life and military life.

When my son turned one year old, I was in officer training and I missed it. That's just one example of how military life is different from civilian life. I hadn't understood that before the Air Force. For example, I'd work all day in the hospital taking care of patients, and then in the middle of the night I'd get a call for a drill: fake deployment. I'd have to put on my uniform and get my deployment bag and go through the stages and be up all night. Then I would work the next day all day in the hospital again without any sleep. It's just a never-ending commitment.

I used alcohol to cope with those sacrifices. But now I realize I need different tools to handle what is expected of me.

*Today I will seek out healthy coping
mechanisms when I encounter stress.*

—Anonymous, U.S. Air Force, 1997–2000

The Reality of My Greatest Fear

I believe that I was built for combat. I did everything at a high speed and in a proficient manner. I don't ever recall stopping and acknowledging my fear. I was able to master it early, and it didn't affect my performance. I was more terrified of how I felt about all I had endured than I was of living in the moment. And those were fears that loomed in my mind.

The best way to describe this is to say I was lost in a cave. Inside there was a candle illuminating. It gave off a warmth that comforted me. But my shadow hovered large; it frightened me and kept me away from the light. My shadow embodied my fears, and the candlelight was acceptance of all that happened. That light burned within me, but all I saw was the shadow.

I made the decision to walk through that shadow and get close to the light. As I got closer, the shadow became smaller. As I worked through all of those fears and traumas of my past, the shadow lost its power. In the end, the light will always conquer the dark.

Today I will believe in the power of the light I have burning inside of me, and I will shine that light in the darkened corners of my past.

—Bradley L., U.S. Army, 2005–2010

Another Seed Is Planted

After I finished a substance abuse rehabilitation program, I was still working with an AA sponsor. I got through Step Three, and he wouldn't let me get past it—we kept reading the Big Book, and I was ready to get this shit out on paper. He wouldn't let me do it. I was a ball of anxiety all the time.

Eventually I fired him as a sponsor and found an old, retired master chief who sat and answered the phones for the Intergroup Council. He became my new sponsor. This started the journey. We did one Step a week. He walked me through all of it, and it was amazing. He's since passed. Bill A., great guy. I'll never forget him.

I will surround myself with people who heighten my commitment, willingness, and growth in recovery.

—Matthew S., U.S. Navy, 2006–Currently Serving

Lifesaver

For me, connection in recovery is a lifesaver. I have a community, and it's all thanks to being able to volunteer. If I am not around, I tend to fall to the background easy; I feel disconnected. Still I have a sense of responsibility and duty. When the SHE RECOVERS Foundation started Zoom meetings, I got involved. I coordinate and cohost meetings once a week.

Like the military, if I have a responsibility I signed up for—hell or high water—I have a responsibility to the community. I am held accountable to those in attendance. I don't want to let them down.

Today I will get connected with a recovery community and be of service.

—Jen O., U.S. Army, 1995–2019

Learning to Deal with Emotion

For those of us who have been numbing ourselves with drugs and alcohol, it can be difficult to know what to do in sobriety when confronted with strong emotions. It was that way for me. From high school until I sobered up, I had been numbing my feelings. I had no adult experience in handling my emotions.

Recovery has given me the strength to look in those dark corners of my mind and face the reality that there are things that need to be addressed. Doing so has made me a better person. Now, instead of ignoring painful emotions, I have learned I need to be brave and open up to them. I've been in therapy, and that has helped, and connecting with other sober veterans has helped as well.

I needed to realize that the way I was processing painful emotions wasn't working. I was just ignoring them. As I've grown in my sobriety, I've learned to adapt to these difficult feelings. I'm not perfect, but I'm working on it.

On this day, I will seek out tools that will help me accept and process my emotions.

—JR W., U.S. Army, 1987–1995

My Life Had Become Unmanageable

Some places call it K2; others call it Spice. It used to be sold in smoke shops, and it can really mess with your mind. I tried it when I got home from Afghanistan and was put in this platoon for people who were getting in trouble or getting kicked out. Drugs and alcohol were pretty typical. I had some really terrible experiences on that drug. I was afraid I was going to be high forever.

Then I was introduced to bath salts—the street drug that affects you like meth or crack. I used it to cope, and it destroyed me. One of the resentments I have is toward my unit and toward the Marine Corps, because people knew I was in trouble and nobody tried to help. No one did anything. And, not knowing then what I know now about recovery, I didn't do anything to help myself. I was addicted. I'd go home and cry, then stay up all night tweaking.

That was then; this is now.

Today I give thanks for having the courage to take the First Step of NA: admitting my powerlessness over my addiction and facing the fact that my life had become unmanageable.

—Berlynn F., U.S. Marine Corps, 2009–2011

Not Just One Way to Get Sober

For a lot of us in the military, AA is helpful, because there are a bunch of rules to follow to get sober. But nowadays, there are other programs, other avenues for recovery—harm-reduction models, church-based recovery, and more. I'm really excited to see all these people getting sober in whatever way works for them.

But one thing that's common among these programs is that you have one person helping another person. There is a community of people seeking sobriety together. When I work with another person in recovery, it helps my recovery, because it keeps me accountable. Then as their sobriety grows, they can help someone else. We are a network, and we stick together.

Today I will recognize many avenues to sobriety, and I will connect with someone else in recovery.

—Sean A., U.S. Army, 2007–2011

Stop Hanging On to Your Ego

If there was something I could tell my younger self, I would say to stop hanging on to your ego—that's gonna get you in trouble. Listen to the people who came before you. Listen to knowledgeable people.

Learn this in the Army: listen to those who know. Pull your head out of your ass, get out of your head, and start listening. Don't try to solve this yourself. You can't.

That's what I would say to myself.

Today I will be open and listen to messages
from the people who know.

—Ed C., U.S. Army, 1975–1979

You Already Know How to Adapt

For many of us, from the moment we enlist, it's a whirl-wind. The pressure is on from the beginning, and all of your decisions have consequences. Everything is differ-ent from your former civilian life. But you adapted. You made it through.

Then you adapted again back into civilian life. You were surprised at how foreign it felt and how hard it was to come home. You struggled to find yourself again, but here you are.

No matter who you are, recovery requires you to adapt and push past your comfort zone. No one would claim it's easy. But remember this: you already know how to adapt. Even if you made mistakes in the past, you are one step ahead, because you have learned from those mistakes. You are strong enough to adapt again and take on these new challenges.

Today I remember how far I've come, how much I've grown. Today I remember I've adapted to challenges before, and I am strong enough to do it again.

—Anonymous, U.S. Army, 2009–2016

Letting Go of Self-Blame

For over twenty-one years, I blamed myself for getting raped by two military police officers. I didn't tell a soul—not even my best friend. I was so ashamed that I drank and found myself in that predicament. That's when my military career started going downhill.

I made the rank of E-5 in less than five years, which is crazy. I was even getting qualified in air traffic control positions at an accelerated rate. But after the incident, I got another DUI. This was on top of talking back to first-class petty officers and showing up late for duty. I had to go to captain's mast and got demoted. For me, that was the worst thing that could happen, aside from going to jail. They also sent me to rehab for thirty days, but it wasn't about saving my life. I did what I needed to do to keep my job. I kept silent and was discharged for alcohol rehabilitation failure.

It wasn't until recently that I was able to release the self-blame I've carried all these years. In therapy I learned that no one has the right to invade my space, to invade my femininity—whether I have been drinking or not.

Today I will continue to let go of self-blame,
knowing I am only responsible for what I do,
not for what is done to me.

—Elora K., U.S. Navy, 1997–2007

Military Commonality

No matter what branch of the military you were in, or where you served at or were stationed at, you all kind of know the same basic things. You know that it's really hard to be away from home. No matter what, you are put someplace you probably don't want to be, doing something you didn't exactly sign up for.

When you get into a group of veterans, everybody in these groups has these things in common, you know. We all lived this for at least a little while, and as a result, we can relate to one another. Sometimes, we have to look at the things we have in common in order to lean on each other.

On this day, I will focus on the similarities
that bring sober veterans together.

—John K., U.S. Navy, 2005–2009

Service Work Keeps Me Going

I have received a lot of rewarding gifts—especially from working with people. After I retired from the Navy, I went to college and got a certificate in addictive disorder studies.

When I worked at the Alano Club, girls knocked on my door and asked to speak to me. I would welcome them and say, "Come on in, and shut the door." I also worked at a treatment center where women lived with their children. The staff taught the women a trade, from day care to cooking and cleaning.

Later, during the pandemic, I served as the secretary of virtual meetings. Soon I am going to switch hats to become treasurer. I enjoy being of service to others in sobriety.

Service work brings inspiration, rejuvenation, and restoration.

—Mary H., U.S. Navy, 1984–2004

The Spiritual Side

For me, "getting" the Higher Power and really understanding God has been my biggest thing. The spiritual side of recovery helps me the most. If you're in a routine where you're doing a self-inventory and living a life with no regrets, then you don't constantly have to be afraid anymore.

Spiritual meditation and prayer also helps, as well as being there for others. Service to others—or just being a nice person—really helps. If you can do that, then you're living a life. You can just show up; you don't have to prepare for every moment like it's game day. You're already just doing it—you're really living a life. That is what we're meant to be doing, just being present in the moment.

My Higher Power helps me with all of this. I don't have to be worried when I attend an event with wine or when I encounter challenges in my leadership role, because I've done the spiritual prep work ahead of time to get through the day.

Today I will put in the prep work needed
to get through the day without fear.

—Guy C., U.S. Navy, 2005–Currently Serving

It's All about Sobriety and Acceptance

I went to gay and lesbian meetings for a long time in the beginning, then I realized it really didn't matter. As long as it was open, people didn't care either way. But I feel most comfortable at women's meetings and talking about sexuality with close friends, my sponsor, or a therapist.

My first sponsor was a woman. After her I had a gay man named James. I felt safe with James as my sponsor because of the sexual assault I had experienced in the military. I didn't want another lesbian as a sponsor, because I didn't yet know then how to be close to somebody without being sexual. For me, it was all about sobriety, and James was a wonderful AA sponsor.

There are a lot of gay, lesbian, and trans people out there committing suicide every day. And many of them are veterans. Finding the right group at the right time can save lives.

Today I pray that my sisters and brothers who struggle will find the help and support they need.

—Deb L., U.S. Army, 1981–1996

Service Is Recovery

In a million years, I wouldn't have ever been able to guess that this is how my life would turn out.

Service is a big part of my recovery. I have to be constantly giving back in order to maintain my sobriety. Participate, actively work the Steps, and have a sponsor. Know and love the literature.

Turn your greatest liability into your best asset. Share your story, because others need to hear it. Leave no one behind.

I turn my greatest liability into my best asset.

—Emil C., U.S. Navy, 1995–1997

I Finally Stopped Running Away

I'm in the VA health care system—I am 100 percent disabled from my time in the military. On top of all that, when I was jumping from ship to ship in the Coast Guard, it turns out I was exposed to radiation, which rendered me unable to father children. Even though I have lots of resentment toward the military, I am still proud of my service in the Coast Guard. It also got me away from my father at the peak of his abuse.

I don't know if I became an alcoholic in the Coast Guard or I already was one, but I sure got addicted to all the booze and stuff we consumed when I was in. When I got in trouble for drinking, I knew it was going to be hell if I stayed in. I'm grateful for a moment of clarity when I had the choice to fight it, or take an honorable discharge and walk out without a court martial or going to captain's mast. I did what I always did—deflect the uncomfortable conversations and situations, and run away.

I finally got sober when I realized I couldn't run away any longer.

Today I'm grateful for that First Step that opened the door to the other Steps. When I quit running and faced the truth of my addiction, I discovered a world of possibility and hope.

—Joe K., U.S. Coast Guard, 1988–1996

Alcoholism Doesn't Go Away

I was in a meeting the other day with a woman who had thirty years of sobriety. But then one of her parents died, and then shortly after that, the other parent died. The woman was suddenly caught up in her grief and loss, and she thought it would be okay after thirty years to have a drink. We didn't see her again for two years. Thank goodness she was able to come back when she did.

So no matter what we do, once we are alcoholics, we can't change back. We need to be vigilant and keep following the formula that helps us stay sober, because when something unexpected and harmful happens, we need to be ready to stay sober throughout that experience.

*Today I will remember that it only takes
one drink to fall back into a bad place.*

—J. D., U.S. Army, 1985–1993/1998–2018

As Long As You're Breathing, There Is Always Hope

I work as a peer supporter at a treatment facility. As much as I would like to recover for clients, I learned from my own experience that they have to do the work themselves.

I'm also an AA sponsor and go to meetings at a VA facility, so I meet a lot of vets my age and also older vets who served in Vietnam. It's an inspiration to connect to these guys and discover that we went through the same combat stuff. It's a great feeling to steer other vets who need help in a direction where they can find like-minded people.

Being a vet is a unique situation, and the suicide rate is something like an average of twenty-two a day for us. As a fellow vet, I can say, "Yeah, it's a long, bumpy ride. I've been there. But don't give up on yourself. As long as you're still breathing, there is still hope."

Today I will practice the lesson of Step Twelve: to keep it, you have to give it away. Today I will offer my hand, heart, and ear to another vet in need.

—Kenneth B., U.S. Air Force, 2001–2007

A Double-Edged Sword

My military service has both helped and hindered my recovery. Let me explain what I mean. The Marine Corps made you tough and taught you how to be self-reliant, disciplined, and how to get things done. But when I was trying to get sober and in recovery, some of those skills made me think I didn't need help, because I was a tough guy.

Sometimes the qualities of self-reliance and commitment helped me power through and get to meetings. I could see that. But also, that same courage and individualism worked against me too. It gave me excuses not to do the work that needed to be done. I would think, *I can do this, I am tough enough, and I don't need to go to that meeting.*

What I'm saying is, what I learned in service was helpful, and it was also not so helpful: a double-edged sword.

Today I will take the lessons of service and apply them to my recovery where they are helpful.

—Mike D., U.S. Marine Corps, 1970–1974

Attitude of Gratitude

When I was about ten years sober, I was having chest pains. My best friend, who is another military guy and also my sponsor, took me to the hospital for tests. They found three blockages in my main arteries. I made a complete surrender to God before they wheeled me to OR, where I had an out-of-body experience and was looking down on myself. And when I woke up in the recovery room, I thanked God for getting me through it.

Ever since then, I feel like I'm on borrowed time. I still start and end each day with prayer. I wake up and thank God for getting me through the night. I slide out of bed and do the first three Steps, and if I need to, I ask for support, guidance, and help for other people in need, and finish with the Lord's Prayer. Then I have coffee while I do my daily readings and reflections. I've been doing that for years now and live the best life I've ever had.

Today I thank God for getting me through another night, and hold all those in my heart who might be in need of his support and guidance.

—Mike F., U.S. Navy, 1959–1965/1972–1990

I Am My Harshest Critic

I found this incredible sponsor who's not military at all. You would think as a military person, I'd want someone who was like me—someone that had a bit of an edge, a huge chip on their shoulder. But that's not what I needed for a sponsor. And God bless her, she knew that.

I don't know if it's being an alcoholic. I don't know if it's just being me. I don't know if it's being a soldier. But no one is a harsher critic of me than I am. I didn't need a sponsor to tell me how I was screwing things up. I would know long before they did. I needed a sponsor who would be able to come in and say, "Hey, be gentle with yourself," and then teach me what that's like.

I didn't know how to do that. She did, and she took me through the Steps. It was incredible, and my life changed. Promises started coming true.

Today I will be gentle on myself when I need kindness.

—Jenna R., U.S. Army, 2005–Currently Serving

Accountability Is the Best Policy

People say, "Oh, I don't need to do that" or "I can get something for somebody, and it's not going to cause a problem in my recovery." If you make that okay, what else will you make okay? Is it going to be okay to have a light beverage? Is it okay to have an O'Doul's? I had to set up parameters for myself that I stayed within—and I don't have any of that stuff in my life today.

I don't want to take a chance. I don't want to risk it. I was in bad shape. I don't want to be that again. I was a drunk. I got sober.

Today I will set and nurture the boundaries
I've set in my life to maintain my sobriety.

—Gayle C., U.S. Army National Guard,
1976–1980/1984

Square Peg

I think something that makes us unique in the military is we know our personal lives are sometimes held against us in the overall structure of promotion and evaluations. Sometimes it can be good. Sometimes it can be bad.

I wasn't the guy that went to all the parties, hung out with all the people who drank, and had friendships with my superiors. I would argue that, to some degree, that worked against me. That's why I probably didn't make chief and officer sooner, because I wasn't at the after-hours functions, rubbin' elbows. I wasn't into bars. Even when I got more senior, I was out doing things that sober people do. As I advanced in my career, I became a living example of authentic leadership while serving in sobriety.

As a square peg dedicated to sobriety,
I'm comfortable with not fitting in.

—Joe H., U.S. Navy, 1988–2015

A Higher Power That Makes Sense to Me

By working my program and developing a healthy relationship with a Higher Power, I was granted the gift of sobriety. I identify as a pagan now, where I see divinity as being present in nature and in the natural world. That's actually the biggest thing that got me interested in AA.

When I was in treatment, one of the guest speakers told us that you can choose your own Higher Power—your own conception of what God is to you. For me, that was my aha moment. Like, *Maybe this can work for me.*

Because of my relationship with my Higher Power, I'm much more thankful now when I have a good day, and I try to be less self-centered when I have a bad one. For me, I don't just ask my Higher Power to help me get through tough times for myself—I ask for help getting me through this struggle so I can be better and more present for those around me.

Today I will look at the ways I have grown more
thankful and less self-centered in recovery.

—Dennis D., U.S. Army, 1997–2003

The Definition of Sanity

It took me a couple decades of drinking in the Navy before I got treatment, but I've been sober now for forty-two years, and the pieces of my life have fallen into place. There are still hard times, but now I have the recovery tools and support I need to get me through them.

And when the time comes, I'm not afraid of dying. I'll be eighty-two, and if I wake up tomorrow, I'll get to do what I did today. If I don't, I get to go be with Jesus. So it's win/win.

If insanity is doing the same thing over and over expecting different results, I guess sanity must be doing the same thing over and over and expecting the same results. I wake up in the morning and ask God to keep me sober. I go to three meetings a week. I try to help other drunks. I sponsor a lot of people and so does my wife. I didn't have a purpose before I got sober. I've got a purpose now.

*Today I give thanks for the life and purpose
recovery has granted me.*

—Bud N., U.S. Navy, 1957–1983

Being Aware of My Triggers

Now that I'm sober, one of the things I need to do is be aware of what triggers my PTSD so that I can avoid episodes. If I am being vigilant of my triggers, I am taking care of myself. For example, I know one of my triggers is fireworks. Recently I was in Mexico, and the place we were staying set off fireworks every night at 7:30. So once I realized that, it was my responsibility to be in our room with headphones on to listen to music or watch a show before that time. I don't want to expose myself to that and all the problems that come from a PTSD episode. I'm in therapy to help treat my PTSD, and that helps a lot too.

I can't control everything that happens in the world. But I do have my tools, like meditation, to help out when I do experience a trigger.

Today I will take steps to be aware of what upsets or triggers me, and develop tools to help me cope with episodes when they do happen.

—Eric S., U.S. Marine Corps, 2005–2009

Like What You See in the Mirror

Most of us fell so far that we lost our sense of who we were. And there was nothing quite as depressing as looking at myself in the mirror. All I saw whenever I looked at myself was a monster that killed with no conscience. And I hated him. Because I was there for every squeeze of the trigger.

In active addiction, I saw how hollow and lifeless my eyes were. I had these dark rings around my eyes that made me look like I was trying to give a raccoon a run for its money. My skin was pale, and I was at least fifty pounds underweight. So I didn't look in the mirror. It was a reminder of how far I'd fallen and all of the good people I'd let down on the way.

Slowly but surely, I got to know myself again. That light in my eyes came back. The only thing I had to change was everything. It wound up saving my life. And it all began with me needing to be able to hold my own gaze in the mirror.

Today I will appreciate and care for the person
I see in the mirror looking back at me.

—Bradley L., U.S. Army, 2005–2010

Family Reunion

The judge looked at me and said, "You're an example of how we want people to come back to court, because people sometimes get their kids back too soon. They end up back here in the same place, because they're not ready to get them back."

He commended me for refusing to have my children returned to me until I was comfortable in my sobriety. In turn, I ended up getting my sons back with no stipulations. We soon moved into our own apartment. A few months later we made plans to move to South Carolina to be closer to the rest of my family.

I hadn't seen my sons since 1986, because I was using, and they hadn't met any of my family members. In 2002, my sons and I agreed to move to the South and reunite with my family. It was one of the most awesome decisions we ever made.

My recovery program not only heals me but also heals the relationships within my family. Today I get to express my gratitude through a living amends.

—Karen A., U.S. Air National Guard, 1980–1991

Sharing Recovery

I've gone through a lot of suffering because of my drinking, but I've been able to put addiction behind me. The thing is, not everyone is ready to hear about the benefits of quitting alcohol.

In fact, as time goes on, some people try to hide their drinking even more. Especially because the older I get, people think I've created this career and I'm successful. Maybe it made sense to have this problem when I was younger, but now that I'm older, I need to hide these issues, because I should be older and wiser, so to speak. I shouldn't be struggling with alcohol still.

These people don't want a recovery evangelist. They may stop looking you in the eye. They may not be ready to hear the message. The key, for me, is just being open about my own recovery. I live in such a way that others can see that quitting has positively benefited my life. I don't preach, but if people have questions, I am right there to support and share.

*Today I will be proud of my recovery and share
the message with anyone who asks.*

—Terry F., U.S. Army, 1986–1994

I Just Accept It

I'm truly honored to wake up in the morning and have positive things happening in my life. Like, I don't have to really work for it. I just do the right thing, and they just happen. That's where it all begins: just start doing the right thing.

I do all this stuff that I learned along the way, but it could be as simple as just waking up, making your bed, setting a routine—something so simple. Develop a routine that is going to give you a check-back in life.

Before, I didn't know that recovery was simple. I know that in my heart today. I keep my life really simple, because I'm the kind of person who can overwhelm myself with just about anything. I'm at a point in my life where I really don't see it as a necessity to have goals to have these dreams come true; just by doing the right thing they come to fruition. It is amazing to me sometimes. I look at these very graciously. I don't try to make sense of it. I just accept it.

> *Today, do the right thing. Then do the next right thing. Then watch your life change.*

—John F., U.S. Air Force, 1985–1996

DECEMBER

Alcohol, the Infantry, and Being Sociable

In 1971, we used to say that the infantry lends color to what would otherwise be a drab, stuffy affair. By that we meant that alcohol was incorporated into our "ceremonies," to put it nicely, at the officers club. If we were drunk and rowdy, they always covered for us.

In my efficiency reports, they have this little box you would check: "Is this officer sociable?" It was supposed to mean: "Is this service member an officer and a gentleman?"

But I was more "sociable" than most, and that was encouraged. In fact, they wanted us to bring this sort of "color" to the infantry. They have a macho image to uphold.

But after the military, veterans who behaved in that same "sociable" way find out no one is covering for them now. Drunk and rowdy behavior has a cost in civilian life. Now that I am sober, I have found a different way to be sociable. Now, instead of being carried drunk out of the officers club, I lift up other veterans—other people who are struggling with a transition back into civilian life.

Today I bring color to my environment when
I lift up others. I am sociable when I share
my story and connect with those who struggle.

—Dan N., U.S. Army, 1971–1977

Rewind the Tape

In recovery I occasionally think or talk about the fun times from my past drinking experiences. Then I remember that it was fun because I was wasted. The gratifying thoughts are suddenly replaced with memories of the slow and shaky hand salute while practicing for Honor Guard, drinking before work and at lunch, drinking just a little bit and blacking out for who knows how long, not showing up for duty, my mouth watering from the thought of a drink, hallucinations, and the constant fear of losing rank or getting kicked out.

It's time to think of something else.

When I think of my destructive past,
I will immediately ask myself,
"Am I glorifying this?"

—Anonymous, U.S. Army, 2005–2009

Standing Up for Myself

When I got back, I was physically injured. I was wounded and had to be on some pain meds for a little bit. For a while. But they gave me more painkillers than you should give a terminal cancer patient. And what I found was that those drugs didn't just heal—like, take care of the physical pain—but they also made it so I was oblivious to the emotional pain. And that is, by far, the thing that cuts the deepest.

I went to my captain before I got out, because I couldn't stop. I was physically addicted. I was going through withdrawals. I went to my captain, my CO, and said, "Sir, I can't just stop taking these pills, like, I'll be sick and I need to go to the psych ward to get off of the medicine." He looked at me and said, "Suck it up, you'll be all right." So, when I came out of the Army, I was strung out. The pills that they gave me quickly turned to heroin, and I went down a long, long, dark road.

Though they overprescribed and they ordered us into situations that no human being should ever be in, I was the one who had to get myself out of the darkness.

I'm here and I'm telling you about it, so I'm proof that I found my way out of that darkness.

—Bradley L., U.S. Army, 2005–2010

The Next Day

I went in on Monday, and I was absolutely terrified of what was going to happen. The creases in my uniform were never sharper; my boots were never as shiny as they were that day.

Command Master Chief: Nobody can figure out what the hell is going on with you.

Me: I had some issues before I came in; DUI, drunk and disorderly.

Command Master Chief: Did you come in on any waivers?

Me: No, Master Chief. I didn't have any waivers that I'm aware of. I just had issues before. Obviously, I failed in this instance.

Command Master Chief: What do you think is the issue?

Me: Well, I don't know. You're the master chief. So how about you come up with a solution and you tell me what I need to do, because I have no idea.
And he did.

Looking back, it reminds me of one of those things we're taught in boot camp—go ask the chief if you need a squared-away answer.

*It's okay to seek a solution when we
don't yet know the problem.*

—Matthew S., U.S. Navy, 2006–Currently Serving

Fitting In

I've done a little soul searching about my time in the military.

When I wasn't on duty, drinking was relevant. Particularly being young and living in the barracks. I needed to drink to fit in. I was a mechanic and worked with mostly men in the military, which can be said about a lot of different occupations. From ceremonies to the grog, alcohol was celebrated.

If I could go back in time and speak to my younger self, I would tell her, "You don't have to partake. You don't have to drink to fit in. It's not where it's at."

Today I gain my sense of belonging
and reassurance in recovery.

—Jen O., U.S. Army, 1995–2019

Writing Is a Sobriety Tool

In the beginning, I didn't want to do any writing. I've since discovered that writing is a useful sobriety tool. Once you start writing, your experience just flows out.

What I've learned is, if I sit there and say to myself, *I'm not going to use drugs because I want to be there for my family,* sooner or later my brain is going to start twisting that, and it's going to become a weaker reason to stay sober over time. Then all of a sudden, I'll make an excuse, and I'll go back to drinking or drugging once again.

I've learned that if I put my reasons to stay sober on paper, they become my truth. That is something that I've stuck with, and it has really worked out for me.

I'm always telling people to pick up a pen and start writing. You won't know what's inside you until you start. I mean, I wrote some stuff that I didn't even know that I knew. I'm like, *Where did this come from? I don't remember that bar!* But it works—better than I ever expected.

On this day, I will write down my thoughts and experiences as a tool to keep me sober.

—JR W., U.S. Army, 1987–1995

Suck It Up

When I was out there drinking and drugging, I wish I had known that I could ask for help. If I had read a book that said, "Yeah, I'm a veteran, I'm a soldier, and I have a problem with alcohol. I have a problem with drugs. And I reached out to my platoon sergeant, who connected me with the resource people who gave me the option to go to treatment," I would have done that in a heartbeat, if I knew I could have gotten help. But I just thought I had to hide my usage.

So I would do a Rule 25 for the Army, and I would say I only drank once or twice a week. No! I was drinking all day, all the time, and they knew it too. That's probably why they also kicked me out, because I wasn't being honest.

Nobody reassured me it's okay to be honest. I just thought, you know, *Do yourself. Be tough. Don't be weak. Suck it up.* And that doesn't work for recovery. You have to ask for help.

Today I will ask for help when I need it.

—Sean A., U.S. Army, 2007–2011

You Can't Change the Past

I wasted a lot of time trying to change the past. Like, I had the opportunity to go to West Point Academy or to join the Army Security Agency, which is the military arm of the National Security Agency. I thought about what my life could be if I had made different decisions. But over time, I've learned to not try to focus on my past. Instead, and I can only implore you fellow veterans, focus on today.

We all only get one past, and we can waste time regretting it, or we can get busy creating a different life today. So you remember the past, because it's a lesson. It's not a life sentence; it's a lesson. Pay attention to what the past taught you, but move forward.

I'm sixty-four, but I still have an infinite number of futures ahead of me based on the choices that I make right now—in this moment, with this inhale. We all have different things that we can do to alter our futures. Which future coalesces into our lives and becomes our reality is up to us. We have the strength and the fortitude to do it correctly, to the best of our ability.

Today I will let go of the past and get busy creating
a different future in my recovery today.

—Ed C., U.S. Army, 1975–1979

Speak Your Truth

If I could go back to my younger self, when she first started dealing with the discomfort of coming home from deployment by drinking, I would tell her to talk to somebody.

Back then I was afraid to express my feelings about what had gone on, so I shut down. Drinking was my way of ignoring what was going on around me. All I really needed to do was open up to even one person.

Do not numb the feelings. Speak your truth to another person instead, and feel the pressure slowly start to release. Opening up to another person, even just one other person, can change your story for the better.

Today I will remember the power of speaking my truth, and keep my mind and soul open to finding the right people to share my truth with.

—Anonymous, U.S. Army, 2009–2016

I Am the Storm

In a firefight, some people hide behind a tree. Some people run away. Some people become frozen with fear. Some people move forward, even if their gut says *Run. Hide. Don't move.* In the rest of my life, I don't want to run or hide. I will move forward. Even when my gut says *no*.

You have seen things that others will never see. You have done things that others will never do. That doesn't make you less than. It makes you more. In war, you see the worst of human behavior: cruelty, savagery, cowardice. But you also see the best: selflessness, kindness, mercy, valor. You get to choose what you focus on now.

What hurts worse than one's own suffering is witnessing the suffering of others and being unable to help them. Perhaps you can help now. You are still a warrior. Use your skills to protect the weak, the old, the children, the powerless.

And the devil whispered in my ear, "A storm is coming."
I whispered back, "I am the storm."

—Don E., U.S. Army, 1967–1970

Alcoholism Is No Joking Matter

I grew up with both parents in a loving, middle-class home. They told me early on, "You have two things against you. You're Black and female." With a mental message of having to overachieve, I excelled in grade school—received As and Bs, was active in various sports and choir.

So I joined the Navy, made rank in boot camp, singing cadences as we marched. I only had one experience with drinking before the Navy and didn't drink again until A School. I began to experiment with alcohol at my first duty station—especially after my best friend's death. I drank to drown my sorrow.

Just weeks after my twenty-first birthday I got my first DUI, and my fellow sailors said, "Everybody drinks; you just got caught." I spent a night in county jail, went to a mandated military class, received a certificate of completion, and returned to work within a week. It was a joke.

But as recovery teaches, alcoholism is nothing to joke about.

Today I am grateful for lessons learned—
even if they're learned the hard way.

—Elora K., U.S. Navy, 1997–2007

We Have a Choice

There are addiction issues in my family. My great-grandfather, my mom, my sister, and my brother all have their own manifestations of addiction.

As for me, I was a motivated kid. I never drank in high school, and I went to the Naval Academy prep school up in Rhode Island at age nineteen. I had my first drink there. In fact, I had four Heinekens, laughed hysterically, and blacked out. From that beginning, once I started drinking, I couldn't stop.

As my drinking progressed, I started to run into more problems. But I was able to get help. My sobriety date is in October of 2018. Despite the fact that my family has a long history of addiction and that I was an alcoholic right from the beginning of my drinking years, I was able to stop and get help.

What makes my story different is the support I received along the way in my recovery. I let people help me. I swallowed my pride to get where I wanted to go. I did not want to lose my flight status, and I'm thankful to say I never did.

Alcoholism can strike any of us, but it's what we do with the problem that matters.

Today I will take responsibility for my choices.

—Guy C., U.S. Navy, 2005–Currently Serving

Getting through the Dark Times

There has been so much good stuff in sobriety, but it's not all roses. There are also some really dark and painful times too.

After the military, about eight years ago, one of my long-term good friends was murdered. He was stabbed to death. That was a heartbreaker. I've been sober thirty-one years and have experienced a lot of other losses too. A couple of my sponsors have died.

But that's life, and we help each other through it. I've got people and tools to help me get to the other side of tragedy. I know how to ask for help when I need it. I've got meetings. I practice mindfulness and meditation and yoga. I read and I journal all the time. I always try to do something spiritual—something for my body, mind, and spirit.

And I try to keep my sense of humor and not always take things too seriously. It's important to be able to cry. But it's important to remember to laugh too.

*Today I will use the tools of recovery that feed
my body, my mind, and my spirit.*

—Deb L., U.S. Army, 1981–1996

Reconciliation and Healing

I decided I had to reconcile my past with the military and finally deal with the military sexual trauma I experienced. I went to the VA to get help. I knew that if I didn't get this help that I would never be able to maintain my recovery.

My therapist said, "You know, what have you got to lose?" I had nothing. I had nothing to lose and everything to gain in that moment, even though I was terrified of remembering the story.

"Assaulted." It was the first time I ever heard it spoken that way. Simple words can mean so much when you've been through something like this.

The process of working with a therapist would allow me to become the person I was supposed to be before any of this shit ever happened to me, before I ever had a drug put in my body, before any of this trauma.

I decided that I would take advantage of whatever they had to offer me to benefit my recovery.

—Emil C., U.S. Navy, 1995–1997

I Don't Want to Get Stagnant

Something that has really worked for me in recovery is staying busy and having good things going on. I have a productive business, I work on my relationship with my daughter, and I focus on acts of service. I try to keep my mind focused on good things happening today and positive things to look forward to.

I struggle with meetings. It can be a challenge to try to talk to other people. It's an awful thing to have an addiction, and it's certainly a sickness or disease. I just keep moving forward and can't stay in just one place. I have to keep moving, or I worry that I will relapse.

I want my sobriety to mean something. I want to have something to show for it. I am not at the point where I am proud of what I have accomplished, but I have hope that I will get there someday.

Today I will think about what motivates me to stay sober, and I will seek those things out.

—John K., U.S. Navy, 2005–2009

Vets Helping Vets / Paying It Forward

My own father is a Vietnam vet, and my recovery and peer support work has helped me help him. He's not an alcoholic, but since I got sober and got PTSD therapy, he's now getting therapy for his own combat-related PTSD. Like a lot of Vietnam vets, he didn't have a high opinion of the VA, so he never got help. But when he saw the difference it was making for me and how happy I was, he started asking me questions about where I went to get help.

We started talking honestly to each other about our combat experiences—about nightmares and triggers and other PTSD symptoms. Next thing I knew, he had set up an appointment for himself. And now he seems so happy—like the weight he's carried for over forty years is finally being lifted.

It's been wonderful. I feel like my journey wasn't only about me. Part of it was about helping my dad get his life back. But every aspect of my daily life is better.

Today I will practice paying it forward by reaching out to offer help to another vet.

—Kenneth B., U.S. Air Force, 2001–2007

It's Never Too Late to Make Amends

I learned discipline in the military. I've learned to apply that to my everyday life and in my recovery program. But there are other vets who never get the help they need because of the stigma of asking for help. You've got to learn to swallow your pride, which isn't easy but is the best thing I ever did. And you need to learn how to make amends.

My parents died before I got sober. We didn't end on very good terms, and when I started working the program, I didn't know how I was going to make amends. My sponsor told me to sit down and write a letter to each one of them and give it to him. And when I got home, I also got on my Harley and went to the cemetery. I went to their headstones and sat on the grass, swallowed my pride, and made my amends with tears running down my face.

Today I'll ask forgiveness of someone who deserves it, even if they've passed, because I've learned it's never too late to make amends.

—Mike F., U.S. Navy, 1959–1965/1972–1990

Emotional Sobriety

The good thing is, today I don't have a mental obsession with drugs or alcohol. But what I do have is sometimes I want to feel sorry for myself and wallow in self-pity. Then I feel as miserable as if I had a real hangover.

That emotional sobriety thing is a real thing—I didn't believe it. I thought it was a bunch of, you know, yoga-like mumbo jumbo. But it's a real thing.

Having some emotional sobriety means making peace with my past so that my past no longer has power over me. How do I do that? By sharing my story with others and by working with other women to share what I've gone through in ways that can help them.

I'm still working on that emotional sobriety thing. But when I'm helping other people—not for an ego boost, but helping them by sharing similar times that I went through hardship and came out unscathed? Oh, wow. That's the only way that I can give myself any semblance of peace.

Today I will seek emotional sobriety by focusing on helping others and sharing my story.

—Jenna R., U.S. Army, 2005–Currently Serving

Service Work Feeds

Over the years, I got to be involved in different events. I went to AA and NA in Portland, and that was really something. I'm currently involved with veteran-to-veteran online support. I met this one fellow about four or five years ago. When finding somebody that's struggling, if I know saying something is gonna help, I share what I can. I find things like that are real, real helpful for me too.

I keep remembering that God has kept me alive. I may not know what the reason is, but there's a reason.

Some days it's really hard; it's just heavy. Still, I know I can help. I know there are more people I can touch with my story of sobriety that I haven't met.

When life gets heavy—when I question my purpose—
I will lend an ear and speak a word of encouragement
to another person in recovery.

—Gayle C., U.S. Army National Guard, 1976–1980/1984

Don't Judge Me

When I joined the Navy, I was very reserved about who I told why I didn't drink. It was a handful of the closest people to me.

While attaining my security clearance, I was asked questions I knew I couldn't be truthful about, because it would affect who I could and could not be in the military, and possibly the outcomes. It put me in a very odd position. I basically had to choose to either be dishonest and say, "That's not important, because I'm not that person anymore," or be willing to say, "I'm going to be honest, and I don't know what's going to happen," which, at that point in my career, I was not willing to do. I felt like everything I had ever been told about my recovery would be held against me because I was being honest.

That's what I always wrestled with—I signed a contract to be an air traffic controller, so therefore my dishonesty was justified, because I knew they'd take my job away. I didn't want to be dishonest, I just wanted to protect my right to achieve what I knew I could and not have my alcoholism held against me.

I'm not a bad person; I made bad decisions
in my addiction.

—Joe H., U.S. Navy, 1988–2015

The Complicated Life of Service

When I was in treatment, a lot of the setup was similar to how the military functions. For example, they had a structured routine. I had to go to different groups and classes at specific times. I had to wake up at a certain time, which meant going to bed at a given time. So it was helpful that I was familiar with that type of hyper-scheduled routine from my time in the military.

But at the same time, I know that my drinking got more intense after being deployed as a medic near the border of Kosovo in Albania. That deployment brought up a lot of fear and uncertainty, and I used alcohol to cope with those emotions.

For me, my military experience was both helpful in recovery and a hindrance after deployment. Like most things, it's not just one way or another.

On this day, I will realize the complicated nature of what makes up our experiences drinking and in recovery.

—Dennis D., U.S. Army, 1997–2003

Alcoholism Is the Great Equalizer

I was twenty-two years in the Navy with ribbons and a combat metal. Young Marines I ran into would look at me with respect, probably thinking, *Wow, look at this guy. He's been there.*

What got me sober was when I walked through the gate in my dress whites, drunk as usual. I had fallen down a few times. My ribbons were torn, and there was puke all over me. When I walked through on this occasion, there was this young Marine who looked like a recruiting poster. He was sharp and immaculate. Instead of respecting me, he turned to the corporal and said, "What do I do with this?" The corporal just shook his head and said, "If he can make it on his own, don't mess with it." So I stumbled away with that "What do I do with this?" playing over and over in my head.

For years, I told myself I wasn't an alcoholic. I was a military professional. I did combat. I wasn't sleeping under a bridge. Then I looked down and saw what the Marine saw—a drunken slob in uniform. I threw my wife and kids away. The only time I contacted other family was when I needed money. I thought, *God help me.* And that's what started me on the road to recovery.

Today when I see someone who hasn't yet opened the gate to recovery, I will show them compassion instead of disdain, remembering I was once that person.

—Bud N., U.S. Navy, 1957–1983

Finding Sober Community with Other Veterans

At the VA, I go to meetings in a group setting, and then I go once a week and have one-on-one therapy.

There are always veterans sitting in the waiting room. It's like camaraderie—you're back together with your military buddies. We all talk like we're still in the military, regardless of which branch. It's great to know that they're there so that I can talk to them. We exchanged info so we can get lunch sometime, but unfortunately we haven't been able to meet since COVID. But I'll talk to them on the phone for twenty or thirty minutes every now and then to catch up and see how they're doing.

Some people choose to get sober in AA. For me, I've found veterans to be a better way to connect, because we've been through similar things and can relate to one another.

On this day, I will seek out sober community with other veterans when I see them.

—Eric S., U.S. Marine Corps, 2005–2009

Meditation for My Fallen Brothers and Sisters

I was a kid without much direction when I signed up. I joined for so many reasons: to straighten out my life, find a purpose, make my parents proud, serve my country, and start building a better life. I had no concept about the depth and strength of the bonds that would form between me and my fellow service members—especially with those I deployed with.

So many of the memories I have in the Army are of being cold and wet and sitting in the dark—bad sleeping conditions and worse food. Some dull moments were made fun by my fellows; traumatic moments were bearable because of those who were there with me.

I have a lot of friends who died overseas and many others who died after they returned. It's hard at times. I am often filled with a mixture of emotions when I think about them: sadness about their death, anger at the military or the enemy, guilt that they are gone and I am still here, and grief for the friends and families that mourn them. I do not want to ever forget them. I do not want other people to forget them either.

Today I will write a story about my friend, tell someone else about a funny moment we shared, do something they enjoyed, and think of them and smile.

—Frank G., U.S. Army National Guard,
1996–2004/2014–2022

A Life Worth Living

You know, so much of my life today is about the attitude of gratitude. I repeatedly say that it's good to be a survivor. When I quit being a victim and became a survivor, I quit needing other things. And the first thing I do when I wake up every day, I try to say "Thank you, God" and keep that attitude of gratitude fresh in my mind. Because I am truly grateful for the life I've discovered in recovery. The Twelve Step programs have saved my life, and it's a life worth living.

I quit being a victim and became a survivor.
I am truly grateful for the life I've discovered
in recovery.

—Doc D., U.S. Army, 1968–1970

You've Got Plans?

I have respect for myself, and you can't put a price tag on that. I didn't respect myself while I was in the military, and it showed. I had too many friends. Today I live and let live. I can accept things. It's like, *Not my monkey, not my circus; that's yours*—and I don't have a problem saying that. I plan today. I plan doing things one day at a time. And then I have to live my day.

I believe in a Higher Power, and he laughs when he says, "You've got plans? So do I. Let's see who wins." I'll take his plans over anything, because this opportunity in sobriety was a gift. Today I believe that anything is possible. This is a God thing.

I know there are miracles. I look out at the rooms and on Zoom and I see the miracles—the people who were broken. That's all we are. When we come into the rooms, we're just broken people. We don't have dreams and hopes; they've all been taken away. Then one day we get them back. We get "better" back.

Today I will trust in God's plan. Today I will trust in today. Today I will believe better is a possibility.

—Stephanie C., U.S. Navy, 1978–1983

Giving Back

When I learned about my purpose in recovery, I discovered I didn't want to work with just addicts or alcoholics. I wanted to work with everybody. I wanted to help that little kid who didn't have a mom, dad, brothers, or sisters. I wanted to help the kid trying to fill that void with external stuff, who was growing up always trying to be a part of somebody else's family.

I wanted to help the moms choosing their lovers over their children—choosing alcohol over their family. I wanted to help the dad who slammed a door on his wife and kid when they were screaming, "Please don't go, please don't go!" I wanted to help them, because that's who I was.

And help them is what I did. It's what I do. I must give back that which I stole, not just from my family but from the world. What I stole from society. I engaged in contributing to what I thought was so bad in the world. The world was broken, and I ended up becoming a part of that. I wanted to change it, so I changed myself.

Sobriety serves as the stepping-stone
to selfless service.

—Armando S., U.S. Army, 2006–2009

Had I Known

"Had I known then everything that I know now . . . " is what they always say. I wish I could tell you that applied in this instance, but I am not sure it's that simple. Because there is no playbook or set of instructions that come ready-made for going to war. And there are no instructions for coming home from it either.

There is no way for you to unremember everything that you've seen and done. There will be nightmares. You will find yourself angry without reason or knowing where it came from. You will be hypervigilant and ultra-aware in everyday situations when you cannot have your back toward the door without feeling the need to be on your feet. And the memories of that place will always be with you. In the end, there is nothing that I can say or do to change the awful things you endured.

What I can tell you is that strong is not the only thing that you have to be.

I will remember that recovering from addiction has a playbook and instructions, and I will use them as I face the memories of my past.

—Bradley L., U.S. Army, 2005–2010

It's Not My Fault

My military sexual trauma happened when I was eighteen years old. I had just gotten into the military—just gotten overseas to Okinawa. I guess I always felt that it was my fault. I didn't know any better. I was drinking when it happened. I invited the person, a Marine, into my room.

Later in life, even when I was using, I just wanted to forget about it. And I'll tell you what, I buried that. I buried that a whole lot. I only just came to terms with talking about it in the last few years, even though I got clean in 2000. It came back out again in 2017, and that's only because I got my military records and started doing my claims. I always just thought it was my fault. That's all. My psychiatrist explained that, even though I was drinking, I had said no. I had to do some Step work to come to terms with it.

When someone forces themselves on you, and you say no, that's what it means.

My healing in recovery comes in all forms.
Sometimes saying no applies to more
than a drink or a drug.

—Karen A., U.S. Air National Guard, 1980–1991

Keep Letting Go of the Shame

We know we have a problem long before we ever think to ask for help. But shame keeps us silent so that it can keep us in addiction.

We worry what other people will think, what the consequences might be, or what the hell we're going to do if we can never use again. That's shame telling us that we're flawed. That we aren't worthy. That we won't make it. Shame will never guide us to a bigger life, because it wants us to stay alone and in the dark.

Call it out, and talk to someone. Call it out, and let it go. It takes time, practice, and patience, but it's worth it. Your life is worth it.

May I remember that I am not the worst thing that I've done. May I remember that my shame is not my truth. May I have the courage to bring my shame into the light and let it go. One step at a time.

—Anonymous, U.S. Army, 2009–2016

Leave No One Behind in Service and Recovery

As I remember it, the phrase *leave no one behind* comes out of armed conflict. When you go into a conflict, you want to know that your team has your back (your "six"). You're going to be there for them, and they're going to be there for you. It's the ultimate trust. It's a sacred obligation. The Army has made this part of our warrior ethos: "We leave no one behind." You will not leave a fallen comrade; this is drilled into you from day one.

It's the same in recovery: if someone is reaching out and wants help, we don't leave them behind. To add on to that, a veteran friend of mine who's got multiple years of recovery says, "I leave no one behind. But I don't put more into their recovery than they do. So I'll call them, and I'll reach out to them. But if they're blowing me off, that means they are communicating to me that they're not ready yet. When they are, I'll be there."

But this idea of being there for one another and helping a fellow soldier—that runs deep in the recovery community and the military community.

Today I won't leave my fellows behind—
in service and in recovery.

—J. D., U.S. Army, 1985–1993/1998–2018

Index

About Hazelden Publishing

As part of the Hazelden Betty Ford Foundation, Hazelden Publishing offers both cutting-edge educational resources and inspirational books. Our print and digital works help guide individuals in treatment and recovery, as well as their loved ones.

Professionals who work to prevent and treat addiction also turn to Hazelden Publishing for evidence-based curricula, digital content solutions, and videos for use in schools, treatment and correctional programs, and community settings. We also offer training for implementation of our curricula.

Through published and digital works, Hazelden Publishing extends the reach of healing and hope to individuals, families, and communities affected by addiction and related issues.

For more information about Hazelden publications, please call **800-328-9000** or visit us online at **hazelden.org/bookstore**.

Other Titles That May Interest You

Shock Waves
A Practical Guide to Living with a Loved One's PTSD

Shock Waves is a practical, user-friendly guide for those who love someone suffering from post-traumatic stress disorder (PTSD), whether that person is a survivor of war or of another harrowing situation or event. Through her own experience, extensive research, advice from mental health professionals, and interviews with those working through PTSD and their families, Cynthia Orange shows readers how to identify what symptoms look like in real life, respond to substance abuse and other co-occurring disorders, manage their reactions to a loved one's violence and rage, find effective professional help, and prevent their children from experiencing secondary trauma. 204 pp.

Order No. 2602

Blind Devotion
Survival on the Front Lines of Post-Traumatic Stress Disorder and Addiction

One woman's startling firsthand account of her struggle to protect her children while facing the man she married, a combat veteran plagued by addiction, rage, and depression born from PTSD. A powerful story of pain and forgiveness, horror and hope, *Blind Devotion* gives voice to the thousands of families who are struggling to heal and to achieve the sense of normalcy stolen by the trauma in their lives. 348 pp.

Order No. 3996